MW01714496

I WON'T VOTE ANYMORE!

A Tale of Passion and Politics

Paul I. Jacobs

For Heather!

Enjoy

Paul

ISBN 978-1-63263-144-2

Published by BookLocker.com, Inc., Bradenton, Florida.

Printed in the United States of America.

BookLocker.com, Inc.
2014

First Edition

Acknowledgments

I'd like to thank

- Loree Rose, who lovingly and patiently coped with me as a less-than-fulltime husband while I wrote this book.

- My editor, Angela Pietrobon, who pointed out unclear passages, unmotivated actions, unnecessary words, and unforeshadowed actions, while gently encouraging me to continue to improve my hard-to-classify work.

- Audrey Niffenegger (*The Time Traveler's Wife*), whose genre-bending work led me to attempt a readable book on Political Science. I haven't yet met her.

- Edward De Bono (*Serious Creativity: Using the Power of Lateral Thinking to Create New Ideas*), many of whose books have influenced me. I met him once but I doubt if he'd remember me.

- All residents of the United States and of Canada, the two countries in which I have citizenship. Some of them I haven't met yet, but I will if I continue to spend winter months in Mexico. What they've said to me in personal conversations, letters to the editor, and "comments" spaces on internet sites has persuaded me that this book is needed.

- The Sea of Cortés Writers' Circle, in La Paz, Mexico, formerly hosted by George Potvin and Ros Oberlyn, which provided me with valuable comments at our weekly read-and-critique sessions, and where some members laughed at the right places more than 60% of the time.

- The fictional characters who allowed me to invent and manipulate them.

- A reviewer of an earlier draft of this book, wishing to remain anonymous, who wrote me, "Dad, 'Chalkboard Monitor' is *so* 20th century'."

I'd like to remind her and others those sections of the United States Constitution that I discuss in this book are "Oh, *so* 18th century."

- The following organizations and people (listed in alphabetical order), who provided comments, suggestions, support and inspiration, but who may not necessarily support my point of view:

Allende Books, La Paz, Mexico (Bruce and Kathleen Bennett, Proprietors)
Men with Books, Vancouver, BC
West End Writers Group, Vancouver, BC
Ulla Behn
Emily Carone
Rudolfo Castro
Alfred Depew
Philip J. Downey
Jan Drabek
Bill Fein
David Gorfein
Paul Headrick
Pandi Hopkins
Ian Housego
Joseph Mark Jacobs
Rochelle Jacobs
Doug Jackson
Len Kirschner
Monica Kling
Joyce Kolodny
Lee Lordeaux
Keith Mabbs
Richard Marquez
Brent McLaren
Renee Morel
Edith Neimark
Ros Oberlyn
Ken Ohrn
Nancy Jo Perdue
George Potvin
Rex
Judy Ristity
Peter Dale Scott
Frannie Sheridan
Meryl Sherwood
Carol Stagg
Susan Starr
Ann Thomson
Jack Tait
Rodney Watson
Susan Weber
Michael Winther
Aaron White
Amber Williams

Contents

Preface

A teenage boy and his father are walking along the beach.

"Dad, why do countries fight each other?"

"I don't know, son."

They walk further.

"Dad, what are 'free elections'?"

"Oh, um, I don't know exactly. Would you like some ice cream?"

"Maybe later. But Dad, why do some people wait in line for hours to vote and others…Oh, never mind."

"No, son. Ask me. How are you going to learn if you don't ask questions?"

First day of class

Most enter the lecture room alone. Others enter in pairs. Some are young, some are middle-aged, and a few are old. Almost all of them *look* older than they are.

They are teachers.

They didn't have time to change their clothes or their weary expressions before coming here after work.

From 5:00 pm to 6:30 pm today, they will also be students.

After enough weekly sessions of this class and others, they will move up a step on the pay scale. They may also earn the right to place "M.A." after their name. The courses are especially designed for them and most aren't hard. They are teachers.

Some recognize each other from previous courses. Benjamin shouts "Yo" to Dusty, who rushes over. They go into an intricate handshake and fist-pounding routine.

"You're looking surprisingly good, given that your Yankees really blew it last year," says Benjamin.

"You had to bring that up?" Dusty smiles and playfully tilts up Benjamin's baseball cap.

"Well, let's sit together anyway."

Benjamin smiles, puts his arm around Dusty and leads them to the second row of seats.

Alice spots Josie, rushes over to her and receives a tight embrace. "Are you still seeing what's-his-face?" asks Josie.

Alice sighs deeply. "There are times *I* can't remember his name either. And other times I *want* to forget it, *and* him. But it's so hard to break it off."

Josie takes Alice's arm and leads her to two empty chairs. They are both startled to see the names *Pia* and *Antoine* in exquisite calligraphy on white cards placed on these particular seats. They look around. Alice points out that every seat has a person in it or a white card on it.

"Is this a fancy dinner party or an in-service course at a second-rate university?" asks Josie.

"Yeah, I know what you're saying. Heard anything about the new instructor at all?"

"No," says Josie, "but he must be some kind of control freak. With a sense of aesthetics."

Josie sits down and motions for Alice to do the same.

"Hey, what's the matter, Alice? Why the glum face?"

"I'll tell you later," says Alice, looking around the room. "If I drop the course. Well, even if I don't." She again scans the surroundings. "Just can't talk here and now."

"Sure, Alice. Whenever."

Emily and Bill saunter in together, holding hands, and quickly choose two seats in the back row. When Emily notices the place-cards, she laughs, shows them to Bill. He tears them up. They both sit down.

Alice points out a sign hung on the front wall:

STARTING A COUNTRY FROM SCRATCH:
Re-Forming the United States of America
Please take your assigned seats

Alice gets up to find *her* assigned seat, but Josie pulls her back. More people arrive, and most head to the back of the room. No one sits in the first two rows.

A man rises from his third row seat. He is perhaps in his mid-fifties. He appears to be very physically fit, yet he moves slowly. As he reaches the front of the room, he seems to pick up energy. He turns to face the class. He looks like he has been crying. They can all see that he forces himself to smile.

The game-changer

"Welcome, everybody," he says, "to a brand new course in our program."

"As you may have heard, Professor Leonard, who was to teach the course you registered for, *Advanced Topics in Classroom Managements*, passed away suddenly two days ago."

Sharp intakes of breath are heard from some.

"I was hurriedly lured out of retirement to replace him. The Dean promised I could teach just about any course I wanted, as long as the State Certification Board approved it for graduate credit. You can see the course title I chose behind me.

"Now, that topic may be a bit dicey. But if they reject it, the appeals process will keep things tied up until long after your grandchildren have completed the course. Taught by someone else, I assume."

He smiles. Nobody else does.

"The course I've chosen to teach is far removed from what I've taught previously, and is unrelated to my hobbies of the last few years, extreme sports and calligraphy."

Still no reaction from the class.

"Okay, let's begin."

Suddenly an attractive, determined-looking woman raises her hand, startling him. He stares at her a moment.

"Oh, of course," he says. "Any questions?"

"I'm Josie. What's your name?" asks Josie.

"I'm Professor Reynolds. My friends call me Rennie."

"This course you want to teach for the first time, Rennie, has anyone ever taught it anywhere before?"

"Not that I know of."

"So, if I don't want to take a course that I don't really know anything about, taught by a guy I've just met, *and* it's not the course I registered for, what are my options?"

"Someone from the Registrar's Office will be here…" Rennie looks down at his watch, "in just a few minutes to discuss your options. And I've got to leave for Professor Leonard's memorial service. But before I go, I want to briefly tell you what I have in mind for the course."

He straightens his posture, slowly scans the faces of the teachers in the class, clears his throat and begins. "In the past couple of years, a number of governments in the Arab world have been overthrown, involved in a civil war, or both. We may be called in to advise these countries in setting up new governments based upon free elections."

The class senses a switch in his manner from that of a chatty friend to that of lecturer with information to impart.

Rennie continues. "Why us? Well, after all, we've been under constitutional rule since 1789! We've had free elections to our House of Representatives every two years! We know how to do it right!

"Or do we?

"In our nation's early years, many groups of residents were excluded from voting in our 'free elections.' And before, during, and after each recent election, we've had demonstrations, media battles, and Supreme Court cases about our procedures."

A well-groomed middle-aged woman enters the room. She and Rennie exchange friendly smiles.

"Class, this is Millicent Albright from the Registrar's Office, here to handle your questions about the shift in the course," says Rennie.

Millicent nods and smiles at the class, then places herself at the side of the room.

Josie glances at the visitor, then focuses in on Rennie to ask him, "What does helping governments in third-world countries have to do with our in-service training as teachers here in the U.S.A.?"

Rennie looks at his watch.

"That's a central question our class will explore in this course, Josie, and I expect you will be one of our lead explorers. Before next week's meeting, I'll send you all an email with more details and a draft of the course outline."

He looks again at his watch.

"Any *absolutely essential* questions that I can answer before I dash out?"

"I don't have email service," says someone from the back. Rennie glances in the direction of the voice and sees a tall handsome young man of about twenty-seven, with incongruous grey patches in his hair.

"Your cable is down?" asks Rennie.

"No, I don't have cable."

"Your internet connection is through your telephone line?"

"I don't have an internet connection. Don't need one, I don't have a computer."

"Millie, could I ask you to work with Student Aid to get a loaner to… What's your name, son?"

"Joseph Cobble. You can call me Dusty."

"Millie, could you get Joe a computer by Friday?"

"Rennie, even if it's free to keep, I don't want a computer," says Dusty.

"Why not, son?"

"I got my family a computer last year. Big mistake," says Dusty.

"My younger sister drove everyone crazy trying to round up more '*Friends*' on Facebook than her real friends had.

"My kid brother used it to play games, 24/7. Not 'thinking' games like chess or FreeCell. Destructive, bloody, killing games. He's joining the army as soon as he graduates high school, and he thinks his video game training will give him a leg up on winning a Congressional Medal of Honor.

"My Mom and Dad both got hooked on watching porn, actually Mom more than Dad. I had to restrict their computer use…"

"Really! What an interesting family! How old are your parents, Joe?"

"Huh?"

"Never mind. For a moment, you just had me reminiscing about my own family. I can see why you don't want a computer in your home. So I'll send you a paper copy by special messenger of what's in the email. Are you willing to review it?"

Millicent starts. *Special messenger! Not out of the Registrar's budget!*

"Of course," says Dusty, "if you're willing to do something for me."

"What's that, son?"

"Nobody calls me Joe. I'm Dusty, okay? Second notice."

Millicent thinks, *Finally Dusty called him on it. Joe, Joe, Joe. You've got to move on, Rennie! He's been dead for 10 years now!*

"It's a deal," Rennie says. "Dusty, I'm sure that if Professor Leonard were here with us today, he'd be pleased to see how we settled a conflict between your family values and the university's routine but sometimes unthinking use of technology.

"And he'll be extremely pleased when I arrive at his memorial service only a half hour late."

He runs out.

Millicent moves to the front of the room.

Motives

"As Professor Reynolds told you," says Millicent, "I'm here to handle any questions you might have about the class change."

Almost everyone's hand shoots up. Josie's is not among them.

Alice looks over at her, startled. She whispers to Josie, "I thought you'd be the first to transfer out."

"Changed my mind," whispers Josie.

Then in a normal voice, Alice says, "Before you got here, Millicent, a student asked Rennie what options we had if we didn't want to continue in a course we never actually registered for. He said you could cover that question."

"I was that student, Ms. Albright," says Josie. "At the time I was skeptical that Rennie could deliver the goods. But he's now shown us his ability to think outside the box, his concern for social issues, and his devilish sense of humor. I look forward to taking his exciting new course."

Millicent thinks *What is this interesting, opportunistic young lady up to?*

She asks the class, "How many agree with the last speaker?"

No hand is raised. No one speaks for an agonizing ten seconds that feels like a full semester to both Millicent and Josie.

Finally, from Alice, "What if you're sick of this whole academic scene and you just want your money back *today*?"

I can relate. But the School of Education can barely stay solvent from day to day. Out loud, Millicent says, "Ordinarily, no problem.

"I could let you transfer to another three-credit course in our program, and under the circumstances, waive the usual change-of-registration fee.

"But unfortunately, at this point all our other courses are completely filled."

Groans from the class.

"Well, except for *Advanced Inferential Statistics in Educational Research.*"

Alice shudders at the thought.

"Right now," Millicent continues, "there's just one student in that class. You'd be able to get almost individual attention."

Alice puts her head down on the desk and moans.

"Would anyone here be interested in that course?"

No responses.

"Well then, any other questions?" Millicent asks. "Perhaps on a *different* topic?"

She sees Dusty raise his hand. *Thank God, he's got smarts*. "Yes, Dusty?"

"How did Professor Leonard die so suddenly?"

"The family sees it as a private matter, Dusty, and isn't releasing any details," she answers.

If I had to spend two hours a week with a class like this, I'd blow my brains out too.

Weirdness

"There's something weird about Rennie," says Benjamin, as he signals for his coffee cup to be refilled. "He tells us 'I was suddenly lured out of retirement' but he gives no further explanation. I have to wonder if he has an alibi for Professor Leonard's time of death. I saw this movie where…"

"Oh, come on," says Dusty.

Alice and Josie pass by, and Dusty waves them over to the table. The women sit down.

"Well, I don't think he's weird," Dusty continues. "Maybe still uncomfortable, still settling into a job he unexpectedly got a few days ago.

"And we've all seen movies… But Rennie weird?"

Dusty waves his finger at Benjamin. "Well, maybe like a Red Sox fan is weird: eccentric, intense about his little hobby, but not like a crazed killer."

"Thanks a lot," says Benjamin.

"Usually, anyway," adds Dusty.

"Well, excuuuse me. I never took Intro to Psych," says Benjamin.

"Were you just talking about Professor Reynolds?" asks Alice.

"Who else?" says Benjamin.

"Well," says Alice, "I've noticed a few odd things about Rennie, like how he persisted in calling Dusty 'Joe.'"

"And," adds Josie, "he talked about Professor Leonard like he was still here among the living, still caring about whether Rennie came late to his memorial service. That sort of stuff. He must have been pretty close to Professor Leonard. Now he's grieving, and you sometimes do odd things after the sudden death of someone you cared a lot about."

Josie stares at her friend Alice, trying to imagine whom in her life she's *really* talking about.

"Even if you murdered the guy who died?" asks Benjamin.

Now the other three look intently at Benjamin.

"For me," says Alice, "the tragic aspect of Professor Leonard's death was that Elliot—you remember Elliot? He was in last semester's class with us? He already took Professor Leonard's course a year ago…"

"The same one we were registered in for this term?" asks Dusty.

"Well, that we *thought* we were registered in, yeah. So, anyway, last week he sold me all his class notes and copies of the class exams for $250."

"Too bad," says Josie. "I also got his stuff from that course. For free. I was going to share it with you, Alice."

"You got it for free?"

"Yes, for free."

"You didn't even pay for the photocopying?"

"That's right. Just had to perform a few sexual favors."

"No, no, you didn't! That's awful," says Alice.

"You're right, I didn't. It *would* have been awful. He's not my type at all. I was just kidding. I wanted to lighten the general mood around here."

Alice reaches out to hold Josie's hand. "Maybe it's just *your* mood that needs lightening."

Sex changes and relative democracy

Rennie stands at the front of the lecture room watching his students arrive. He looks at his watch.

"Welcome back. Has everyone here received the course outline I emailed?" He looks over at Dusty. "And Dusty, did you get it too?"

Dusty gives him a thumbs-up signal.

"If you've read the outline, are any comments, suggestions, or questions about it?" asks Rennie.

No response from the class.

"Well," says Rennie, "I'll quickly run through the course outline and maybe a few questions or comments will come up."

He begins reading from his notes:

"STARTING A COUNTRY FROM SCRATCH: Re-Forming the United States of America."

"The Constitution developed in the 1700's may have been adequate for its time. But major changes in the United States, and certainly the world, have occurred since then. Has our process for choosing our lawmakers through 'free elections' kept up with these changes?"

Some students shrug, others text friends, and a few listen intently. He continues reading.

"In 1776, the first House of Representatives had a total of sixty-five members for all the thirteen states.

"Each House member represented about sixty-one thousand voters. Quite a caseload! And, more importantly, he (they were indeed all men) didn't have any internet surveys or even telephone polls to tell him what the people he represented thought about the issues. Or even what issues mattered to them."

"Has that 'all men' really changed much over the years?" asks Emily.

"Good question," replies Rennie. "And it might be a good topic for a term paper."

"Yes," says Benjamin, standing up and adjusting his baseball cap. "If I chose that topic, my title might be 'Sex Changes in the House of Representatives over the years.'"

A few scattered giggles among the students, then whispered comments with those seated near them, and finally almost everyone is laughing, including Rennie.

Benjamin's face alternately shows a puzzled look and a forced smile, like a blinking human neon sign.

"And the body of my report," Benjamin continues, "could be, in 1776, no women in the House of Representatives; but, in 2012, 20% women. That's my guess. End of report."

The class turns to Rennie, awaiting his reaction.

"You might," says Rennie, "present data for every twenty years from 1776 to 2006, discuss what events and factors may have led to changes in the percentage of women in the House, and discuss how the situation in the U.S. has differed from that in the legislatures of Canada, Great Britain, France, and other relative democracies."

A stunned silence.

Then, from Benjamin, "Are you calling the United States of America a *relative* democracy?"

"Would *you* call it an *absolute* democracy?" says Bill.

"Here's my understanding of the situation," says a student nobody has ever really noticed before now. "In the U.S., we allow temporary workers into the country because they have special skills that are desperately needed here. Like, they can do farm work for long hours under a broiling sun for minimal wages without complaining, and our native-born citizens don't have that skill.

"So it works out well for everyone, a win-win situation.

"But after a while the temporary worker gets lonely. He wants to bring his wife, his kids, his parents, grandparents, aunts, and uncles, and cousins and so on over here. So it's no longer one good worker with special skills we're getting, it's a big extended family that over time can outnumber us.

"And that's what *I* understand by the term 'relative democracy.'"

"That's a very interesting interpretation of the term," says Rennie. "What's your name, son?"

"Gregory."

"And what do you teach, Greg?"

"Me? I teach English as a Second Language to adults in evening classes."

"And do your views about 'relative democracy' come from observing and talking with your students in class?"

"Definitely. And outside of class too. I like to get to know them as individuals, make them feel at home here, answer any questions they have about adjusting to life in their new country."

Rennie sees Bill squirming in his seat.

"Bill, do you agree with Greg's interpretation of the term?"

"Well," says Bill, "to me, a *relative* democracy protects *basic rights* like freedom of speech, the right to vote in elections, and the right to practice any religion or no religion, *more than* most other countries do.

"I don't think there are any *absolute* democracies."

"I remember reading about something like this in Canada," says Antoine. "Some immigrants got expedited visas so they could use their 'special competencies' to work in strip clubs or massage parlors, or with clients of escort services."

"This is amazing," says Rennie, "how merely reviewing a course outline produces so much interest, emotion, and understanding in students." *And reveals such ignorance, bigotry, and misunderstanding.*

He wipes his brow.

Catching up

She leans across the coffee shop table.

"What's it like, being back in the saddle?" she asks.

"Well, I forgot there are so many dim bulbs," he says.

"There always are."

"I know."

"But *you* can turn them up a notch or two."

"There are a *few* I feel I'm reaching now, or may reach by the end of the semester anyway."

"Any I might know?"

"Maybe Emily, Bill…"

She nods. "How about Dusty?"

"He's a good kid. He's more mature than other students in the class who are much older. And he's interested in learning!"

She nods again. "Josie?"

Rennie pauses a moment. "She's a breath of fresh and also foul air," he says.

She smiles.

"Anyway, I'm getting a regular paycheck now. Thanks again for your role in making it happen."

She smiles.

"How's Gerald treating you?" asks Rennie.

"Same as ever." The thought of him brings her back to the present. She looks at her watch. "I've got to be going."

"Sure. Maybe next week or so you'll have more time and we can go riding. Have a drink together."

She frowns. "You drink now?"

"Just a little. Sometimes around mid-day I need a little pick-me-up."

Her frown deepens. "You remember…"

"Yes, I do."

She forces a smile and stands up to leave.

"Take care, Rennie."

"See you, Millie."

Do we need to know these numbers?

Rennie stands at the front of the lecture room as his students return to class.

"I said before the break," he begins, "that the first House of Representatives in 1776 had a total of sixty-five members for all the thirteen states.

"Then, in 1910, when the population was estimated at ninety-two million, Congress fixed the membership of the House at its current size, at four hundred and thirty-five."

Some students furiously take notes.

Benjamin takes a different approach. "Do we need to know these numbers on the final exam?" he asks.

"This is only the second week of the semester," says Rennie. "I'll discuss the final exam in two more weeks at the earliest." In his head, he adds, *you're all in for a big surprise!*

Students who have not been keeping notes now start to get out their pens and notebooks. Dusty takes out his pocket calendar and circles a date in red.

Rennie continues, "The four hundred thirty-five members of the House are now spread across fifty states. That's an average of eight and seven-tenths of a representative per state. At the present time, no state is known to have seven-tenths of a representative."

A few smile, but the note-takers write even faster.

Rennie looks down at *his* notes.

"In the country's first hundred years of existence," he reads, "the ringing of telephones was not heard in the White House. A letter from New York City might take fourteen days to reach Philadelphia."

One teacher is overheard saying to his neighbor, "I think it starts with an 'F,' not 'Ph.'"

"Since those days," says Rennie, "we've seen enormous technological growth. For example, the internet lets us send messages around the world almost instantly.

"And perfectly spelled," he ad-libs. "But it's a mixed blessing. I hate all the junk mail I get daily. And I can't return it in a postage-free envelope!

"But aside from my personal annoyance with electronic junk mail…"

"It's not just you, Rennie!" shouts out Dusty. "That daily dose of junk mail helped me decide to trash my computer."

Rennie mumbles to himself, "*Not just me*." He turns his notes face down onto a nearby desk.

"Let's hear from more of you about how the rapid growth in technology has affected your lives," he continues.

"I get a kick out of it every time an instant replay on TV shows an umpire made the wrong call," says Benjamin.

"I've learned the hard way to avoid computer dating," says Josie. "My results have run from awful to disastrous."

"I'm sure you could tell us some interesting and instructive stories," says Rennie.

General laughter, in which Josie joins in.

"But," Rennie continues, "Let's focus now more on how the rapid growth in technology has affected the behavior of nations, and less on personal matters.

"Well," says Bill, "I'm very disturbed by the behavior of our own nation, listening in on our private telephone conversations and reading our private emails. I see all that as an improper use of our technological growth."

Gregory scowls and looks around him at the rest of the students.

"But Bill," he says, "the President has explained that those things must be done to uncover potential threats to our country.

"It's a matter of national defense in a time of war like this. We use these technological advances in electronic eavesdropping to save American lives!"

"Gregory, you used the phrase, 'In a time of war like this,'" says Rennie. "Do you all remember the Constitution gives *Congress alone* the power to declare war?"

A lot of head nods and calls of "yes." A few "yes sirs!" from the veterans in the class.

"Well," continues Rennie, "we haven't declared war on anyone since World War II."

"As I remember," says Bill, "the government never admitted carrying out these electronic eavesdropping activities, until some low level employee leaked it on the internet and supplied documents to back up his statements. I consider his action a proper response to an improper use of our technological growth."

"I've read about countries in a civil war that don't allow outside journalists, and even prevent journalists within the country from reporting on the war, and severely punished those who try to," says Emily. "Often the rebels, who have received technical training or trained themselves, smuggle out their reports on electronic tapes, on DVD's, and through encoded emails."

"Last week you told us the State Certification Board would have to approve this new course as worthy of graduate level credit," says Jim. "Or words to that effect."

Rennie smiles. "Yes, I did."

"You made light of it, like it wouldn't be a real problem," says Jim.

"I may have been a little flip in how I expressed it. You know, it was the first day of class for me as well as for you, and I didn't want to be seen as a stand-offish professor. I…wanted to be liked."

Rennie thinks, *If only Millie could have heard me say that.*

Jim smiles. "Nothing wrong with that, Rennie," he says. "Actually, I suspect you and I share a similar view about the stupidity of war for solving disputes."

"But we must be prepared to fight if our basic interests are threatened," Gregory says.

"Our basic *economic* interests?" asks Jim.

Alice says, "And I thought you were being flip because, and I may be out of line for saying this, but I thought you were still in shock over Professor Leonard's sudden death."

"Yes, I was. And you aren't out of line. I like to feel there's always a place for expressing personal feelings in my classroom," replies Rennie.

Josie says to Alice, "This class has possibilities…"

"But," Rennie continues, "I do want to go on now to discuss the Course Outline, what I hope we'll be able to work on together this semester, and some housekeeping rules."

"Maybe not," whispers Josie.

"I could be talking about other topics, such as environmental and human rights issues, which were often ignored in the teaching of our country's history when I went to school," says Rennie. "Was that your experience when you went through school?"

"Environmental and human rights issues? No, not taught in my school," says Alice.

"Mine either," says Dusty. "Unless I was out that day."

"We had a lot of units and study groups on that sort of thing," says Bill. "But I went to a private school. And we didn't get into stuff like that until well into third grade."

"This private school, Bill," says Josie, "what planet was it on?"

"Let's take a ten-minute break. When we come back," Rennie says with a twinkle in his eye, "I'll be extremely serious."

Is this course for you?

"Here's the central question we'll pursue in this ground-breaking course," says Rennie when they resume. "Should we *patch up* our system of government to deal with all of the major increases in population and area, scientific and technological advances, wars, new international alliances, etc., that have happened in the world since 1776?

"Or, would it be more fruitful to *design* a new system of government for today's (and tomorrow's) United States by starting from scratch?"

"That's a great question," says Alice.

"We will look closely at how we choose our House of Representatives," says Rennie. "*Now* we use elections. But is that a good system? What problems does it present? What might be a better system?"

"A great set of questions," says Dusty.

"We'll focus," says Rennie, "on how we might change our current system, how to evaluate our changes, and how we can then apply what we've learned to help other countries when they set up *their* governments.

"But why should you take this course?"

"I'm beginning to wonder," says Josie to Alice, perhaps a bit too loudly.

Rennie glances at Josie.

"What is *your* role as educators?" he asks. "To pass on *information* to the younger generations you teach? Or is it to give them the motivation, tools and support to critically analyze *how we do things now*, and *explore what we might do differently?*

"And what is *my* role as a trainer of teachers? Is it to pass on the traditional teaching techniques that bored me in all my classes from primary through graduate school? Or can I *break* the chain?"

Josie thinks, *So he was bored too? That's promising.*

She says nothing to Alice.

"I'll touch now on a few topics you might expect in a traditional course outline," says Rennie.

"First, the course activities. I will talk and give assignments.

"You will read, discuss in class, and role-play.

"I will listen, frown, and smile."

"Will you listen, frown, and smile in equal amounts?" interrupts Josie.

Rennie starts to frown, then smiles broadly.

"I'll *always* listen, frown maybe ten percent of the time, and smile ninety percent," he says.

Josie giggles.

"You will each write a term paper on a topic we agree upon," Rennie continues.

"You will also give an informal talk on the substance of your paper."

"Can we work together with another student on the term paper and the informal talk?" asks Alice.

"You can, but in my experience it will be better for you if you don't. Sometimes when two students collaborate on a project, they divide the tasks so that each one does what they do best, and they don't develop further in their weak area.

"For example, let's suppose you and Benjamin decide to work together."

Alice shudders visibly at the thought.

"You, Alice, might utilize your considerable talent in public speaking."

Alice seems dubious, but her expression is hard to read.

"And Benjamin might use his considerable, well-developed skill to bring in baseball analogies at the drop of a fly ball."

Appreciative laughter and scattered applause.

Rennie smiles and goes on. "The class members will role-play a college-educated audience that knows nothing about the topic. A warning that those members who pretend too hard may be encouraged to repeat the course."He looks down at his watch. "Okay, let me quickly read through these final remarks:

"Grading: At the final class meeting, you will submit to me in a sealed envelope the grade you deserve. That is the grade I will give you.

"Questions: If you have any questions about this course outline, please bring them up now or at our next class meeting.

"For a more thoughtful answer from me, please email your questions to me in advance.

"For a superficial answer, please submit them in multiple-choice format.

"Classroom Decorum: Differences in opinion and points of view are likely to emerge during the course. Be courteous to your classmates.

"Be gentle with me, too. It's the first time I'm teaching this course."

He smiles. "Finally," he says, "humor is permitted."

We tell *you* our grades?

Rennie stands at the front of the lecture hall watching his students arrive for the next class meeting. He looks at his watch.

"Welcome back. Has everyone here received the course outline I emailed?" He looks over at Dusty. "And Dusty, did you get it too?"

Dusty gives him a thumbs-up signal.

"Anybody have comments, suggestions, questions?"

"I do," says Dusty. "Just one thing, Rennie. Maybe everyone in the class has the same question, but nobody else wants to ask it?" He looks around the room. "Okay, here goes. You're not serious about giving us the grades we *tell* you we deserve, are you?"

"Completely."

"That's hard to believe."

"I did this once before. It worked just fine."

"Wow! I'll bet there were no complaints."

"Not from the students."

"From whom?" asks Josie.

"The Dean. He fired me."

Startled expressions and gasps from the class.

"And yet you're setting yourself up, to get fired again by the new Dean!" Alice exclaims.

"It's not a new Dean," says Rennie. "It's the same one."

Rennie shrugs. "I doubt if he'll fire me again. He hired me quite recently when Professor Leonard died.

But if he does. . ." He shrugs once more. "I've got to do what I feel is right.

"Any other questions?"

Dusty whispers to Benjamin, "Do you still suspect that Rennie murdered Professor Leonard?"

Benjamin blushes.

"I wonder," says Emily, "why you picked the election of the House of Representatives for us to focus on. Isn't the Senate a more prestigious and powerful body? And of course the Presidency is even more so."

"Good question," Rennie replies. "The answer is that every two years *all* 435 members of the House, but only about 33 of the 100 Senators are up for re-election. So we can gather a lot more information by studying the House elections. And we may learn things that we might then apply to analyzing the Senate and Presidential elections."

"Well, I didn't major in Poli Sci or anything," says Benjamin, "but I know *we* don't vote for the President directly. Some electric college does it for us. I think it's called the E-College for short."

"I actually didn't know that, Benjamin," says Rennie. "Thank you."

I wonder what grade he'll ask for. And what I'll do.

Surprises

A few weeks later, Rennie is talking about political parties when Bill and Emily enter late, take seats in the last row, and surreptitiously hold hands.

"Why do political parties play such a large role in our election process?" asks Rennie. "The Constitution doesn't even mention them."

Bill turns to Emily and speaks softly, "That's a bit surprising, n'est-ce pas?"

"Speaking of surprises," she whispers back, "I didn't know you were so fluent in French. How did you learn it?"

"Well, uh, I used to sleep around with foreigners."

"Used to? And now?"

"Well, I don't meet so many since I acquired multiple citizenships."

She withdraws her hand. The lecture continues.

Who votes, who runs, and who counts?

Rennie finishes adjusting the focus on a computerized slide projector he's brought to class.

"In some very small towns in New England," he says, "residents may still gather regularly to decide issues at town meetings open to all.

"But the nation's more than 330 million residents are far too many to get together to decide anything. So we elect the 435 members of our House to make our laws. Our Constitution leaves most of the election details up to each state. This slide shows all that the Constitution says about the topic:

"No Person shall be a Representative who shall not have attained to the age of twenty five Years, and been seven Years a Citizen of the United States, and who shall not, when elected, be an Inhabitant of that State in which he shall be chosen." Article 1, Section 2

"The Times, Places and Manner of holding Elections for Senators and Representatives, shall be prescribed in each State by the Legislature thereof; but the Congress may at any time by Law make or alter such Regulations, except as to the Places of chusing Senators." Article 1, Section 4

"Not a model of clear writing," says Alice.

"And 'chusing' Senators?" says Josie. "The spelling sucks."

"That's a weird font, man," says Benjamin.

"You think?" says Rennie. "Actually, that's what first got me interested in calligraphy. But I'd really like to chat with you about it at some other time.

"Now, I'd like each of you to raise your hand each time you *agree* with an alternative answer to my next two questions. And Josie, would you please tally the class's responses?"

She smiles and nods.

"First of all, who gets to vote?

"Citizens still patiently waiting in line when the polling station closes?

"Citizens not convicted of a major crime in the state where they now live?

"Citizens who bring a Costco photo ID credit card to the polling place to prove their identity?"

Several teachers remove credit cards from their wallets and wave them in the air.

Rennie goes on. "And who gets to be a candidate on the ballot?

"Those who have won a primary election of the party they joined a month ago?

"Those whose citizenship was challenged in a still unresolved court case begun three years ago?

"Those whose petition signatures were gathered by a company that was fined $300,000 for illegal procedures last year?

"Each state, and sometimes the local community, fills in these gaps, relying on state and local law, precedent, and improvised unwritten 'regulations' for unanticipated situations to decide on these matters.

"Frequently, disputes are brought before the Courts, which 'settle' them well after the election has taken place. The losing side, usually the poorer of the disputants, abandons the now irrelevant appeal process. After all, appeals cost money.

"This gives the major political parties a prominent role. These parties control the selection of judges who interpret the state law, and they also provide the election workers who do the improvising.

"And remember, the word 'party' isn't even mentioned in the Constitution."

Bill whispers to Emily, "And I thought getting the Board of Education to do anything was difficult."

Emily reaches over and squeezes his hand.

"Can we expect questions like these on our final exam?" interjects Dusty.

The students become quiet and lean forward to hear the answer. After all, they have been promised this moment.

"No," says Rennie.

"First, remember that the Constitution leaves these questions up to each state, and the states often disagree on their answers.

"And a newly elected state legislature sometimes decides to change that state's earlier position, and sometimes the courts force them to.

"And finally, if you carefully re-read the course outline, you'll see no mention of a final exam. That's because there isn't one."

Someone in the back of the room claps once, joined by someone in the front, and now all are on their feet. The applause is loud and sustained.

Alice turns to Josie. "And to think I was ready to drop this course."

Now Bill reaches over to squeeze Emily's hand.

Everyone forgets the tallying of responses and the meaning of the results.

What's the use?

Rennie brings the class to order and reminds them of last week's session. "We ended with a discussion of who can vote and how the candidates get on the ballot. Any questions?"

No response.

"Sometimes it's hard to ask the first question," he says. "Who would like to ask the second question?"

A few nervous laughs. Josie, in the front row, stands up. She takes a deep breath.

"You've been feeding us interesting information and I realize we're getting in-service credits for being here, and that it's a step toward a salary increment, but I teach fifth grade, and, well, how am I supposed to *use* this information?"

In the back, Emily whispers to Bill, "I'd really like to get to know her."

Rennie leans forward and squints to read the questioner's name tag.

"Well, let me ask you, Josie, does your school have a Student Council?"

"Yes."

"And your class has a representative on it?"

Josie nods.

"How is the class rep chosen?"

"We vote… I think I see where you're going with this."

"And how do the candidates get on the ballot?"

"Well, I call for nominations, a couple of kids raise their hand, I call on the one who's jumping around less, that kid names either his best friend or biggest enemy, then I call on the other jumper who's wagging her fingers in my face, and we've got our ballot!"

"Then you hand out slips of paper and each kid privately writes down their choice for rep?"

"Are you kidding? We ran out of school supplies weeks ago."

"So what do you do now?" asks Rennie.

"I say, 'Raise your hand if you think *this* kid should be the class rep. Now raise your hand if you think *that* kid should be the class rep. Dexter! You raised your hand twice!'"

"'What's the diff, Ms. Josie?' Dexter will say. 'It cancels out.'"

"Do the rest of you use a similar procedure to pick the class rep?" asks Rennie.

He sees head nods and hears a chorus of 'yes's.

"Anyone use a different method?"

Benjamin calls out from the rear. "I just choose the trouble-maker I most want to get rid of two hours a week."

Rennie thinks to himself, *Ah, yes. Free elections, the essence of democracy.*

And we elect our president *how*?

"Compared to electing the President of the United States, the process of electing a member of the House of Representatives in Congress is simple," Rennie says to open the next class meeting.

"A candidate for Representative will run in one particular election district of a particular state during a *primary* election to become the official candidate of his or her party.

"If successful, the candidate will then run against the other major party's official candidate for the same election district in the 'general' election in November.

"The two major parties are almost always the Democrats and the Republicans. Of the two, the major party candidate with more votes becomes that district's Representative in Congress.

"To keep it simple, I'll ignore for now what happens with 'third' parties and their candidates. Most voters do too. In fact, most voters ignore *all* elections in many states and districts."

"So it's like in Major League Baseball," says Josie. "The regular season and the play-offs together are like a primary election, and the World Series is like the general election."

Benjamin and Dusty look at her carefully, each wondering if she roots for the same team they do.

"Excellent," says Rennie. "I wish I had thought of that myself."

"I wish he had, too," mutters Benjamin to Dusty. "Then I might have followed what he was saying for the last fifteen minutes."

"When you compare the regular baseball season and playoffs to a primary election, and the World Series to a general election," says Alice, "that's a useful analogy. I think it would also apply to professional football, basketball and hockey leagues.

"But one way the analogy breaks down is that professional athletes are often subject to random drug testing. I don't think political candidates are, but I think they should be."

"Excellent point," says Rennie. "And that could be a very interesting topic for your term paper.

"I'd like to turn now to the greater complexities of electing a President.

"First, in the primary election, the voters do not vote directly for the presidential candidate they want to win. Instead, they vote for an *elector* of the *same party* as the candidate they want to win.

"The voters of each state choose a number of electors, the number based more or less on the state's population.

"Then the complexities get compounded. You can read the details in any standard textbook. You probably were already unwillingly exposed to these details in high school."

"This discussion reminds me," says Alice, "of some good advice I once got from an investment consultant. An honest one, who told me not to invest in any financial product I didn't understand.

"It makes me wonder why we have a system of government and elections we don't understand, and what we can do about it."

Let's look under the hood

"Today," says Rennie, "we'll look at the state of Virginia's primary election on March 6, 2012, when registered Republican voters will choose among the electors pledged to the various candidates for the Republican candidate for President.

"Here's my list of the major contenders to be the Republican Party's candidate for President at this moment.

- Michele Bachmann, Minnesota Representative
- Newt Gingrich, former House Speaker
- Jon Huntsman, former Utah Governor
- Ron Paul, Texas Representative
- Rick Perry, Governor of Texas
- Mitt Romney, former Massachusetts Governor
- Rick Santorum, former Pennsylvania Senator

Any comments?"

"Seems to me like a list of somebodies and former somebodies," says Josie.

"Including some with unpresidential-sounding first names like Newt, Mitt, and Rick," says Benjamin.

He turns to his friend. "Maybe *you* should run as 'Dusty Rhodes, former computer owner.'"

"I'll consider it," says Dusty. "Maybe the days of Ron, George, and John are over."

"Michele Bachmann, Jon Huntsman, and Rick Santorum did not submit petitions for the Virginia primary," says Rennie. "I imagine they prefer to spend their campaign funds and make campaign visits in other states where they will see more payoff."

"How many signatures do you need to run?" asks Dusty.

"In Virginia, ten thousand," says Rennie. "Some states require fewer. You could shop around. And some states have rules that all the signers can't come from just one or two counties."

A cell phone rings for the first time in the course. Rennie has never announced that all cell phones should be off. He never thought he'd need to. He is, after all, teaching responsible educators who understand the etiquette of these situations.

The ring is to the tune of "Deep in the Heart of Texas." Rennie glares in its direction. A tall, sunburned man sitting in the middle of a row answers the call. Within seconds, the man gets up to leave. In his rush, he steps on other teachers' feet and squashes their paper-bagged dinners. As he reaches the end of his row, he sobs.

He runs out of the room.

"Why is that man so upset?" asks Alice.

"Who is he? Where's he from? I can't recall him ever saying anything in class," says another teacher.

"From the ring chime of his cell phone, I'd say he's from Texas," says Arthur.

"Texas has the second most electoral votes of any state," says Jim. "It's a rich state, and I'm sure that as Governor, Perry was able to get a huge amount of campaign contributions from those oil billionaires I read about. Maybe something happened to the Governor, and that's why the guy was so upset?"

Another cell phone rings. Rennie is furious. All eyes look around to find the source, and eventually rest on Rennie. He blushes, picks up and answers his phone, listens a moment, and says to the class, "Sorry, I must take this. I'll be back as soon as I can." He starts to leave.

"It's okay, Rennie," Josie calls out after him.

"Shit happens."

"But why did he run from the room?" Jim speculates. "He may have wanted more information about what went wrong. He might be a friend, relative, or heavy contributor to Governor Perry's campaign, or maybe the guy just wanted privacy," "It's hard to know. I didn't even recognize him as *being* in the class."

After ten minutes, Rennie returns.

"Sorry about that interruption," he says. "That call was from one of the few friends I have left in academia. She told me…"

The teachers exchange raised eyebrows and glances when he says 'she.'

"…about an important development in the situation in Virginia we were discussing. Governor Rick Perry of Texas, a candidate we expected to be on Virginia's Republican Primary Election ballot, will not be.

"He did not have the required 10,000 valid signatures on his petition. He submitted 11,253, but enough were disqualified for one reason or another to bring him below 10,000."

"If he couldn't get enough valid signatures, his campaign manager or staff might be to blame," says Arthur.

"Well, maybe 11,253 petition signatures might be enough to provide 10,000 valid signatures if the candidate himself is from Virginia, but Perry isn't," says Rennie. "And many people in this country don't really like Texans. So the Virginia election officials *might* have more closely scrutinized the signatures by the Texan candidate.

"Let's all take some deep breaths now after this disturbance," says Rennie. The teachers calm down a bit. Gradually individual voices can be heard.

Emily says, "If he can't handle his *own petition*, how could he manage the *whole country*?"

Bill asks no one in particular, "If his *supporters* can't even leave a room without stepping on people's toes, can you imagine how his *diplomatic appointees* would behave?"

"You're right, Bill," agrees Arthur. "I know the University charges students from other states higher tuition, but I think they also need to screen them better for politeness."

Return of the Texan

The teachers drift into the lecture room. They are surprised to find the Texan who left abruptly the previous week now at the front of the room, poised to talk with them.

Rennie is seated in the front row, off to the side.

"First, I'd like to apologize for leaving my cell phone on during last week's class, and for making a sudden departure that was physically painful for some," says the Texan. "This is an apology, and not an excuse for what I did or failed to do. There is no excuse."

"What's your name?" asks Josie.

"Rodney."

"Please continue, Rodney," says Josie.

"Thank you, ma'am.

"I have been committed for some time to Texas Governor Rick Perry's bid to become the Republican nominee for Presidential Candidate in this year's election.

"I was also a very minor contributor to his campaign fund. Not all Texans are rich, and I, like most of you, live on what I earn as a teacher. And spur-of-the-moment trips, such as the one I took this past week, are very expensive.

"I flew home to Texas to find out what I could about how the Governor's plans for entering the Virginia primary suddenly got derailed.

"When I got home, I sought out a lot of people I've known and worked with over the years on local political matters. I asked them what went wrong for our

Governor in Virginia. Nobody could agree. Everyone pointed a finger at somebody or something else.

"So I flew back here to our university town. On that long flight I remembered that Rennie told us this course would be focused on how we elect our House, not our President."

Rodney looks over and nods at Rennie, who smiles back.

"Rennie also taught us that the Constitution is vague about the details of how a candidate gets on the ballot, and who is allowed to vote. So each state makes up its own rules, and sometimes improvises on the spot when a new situation comes up. He also told us that it's hard and also costly to get a court to overturn a state's decision.

"So I decided, during a long stop-over to change flights in Chicago, that I would write my term paper on explicit national standards for who can vote and who can get on the ballot for *any* federal election.

"The evening I got back I called Rennie to apologize for my behavior and tell him my thoughts. He asked me to talk to the class today.

"So I'd like to apologize to *everyone* now. If you're angry with me, I hope your anger will subside; if I hurt your foot, I hope the physical injury has subsided and heals quickly. And if you might be interested in working with me on my term paper, please let me know. Thank you."

"I accept your apology," says Arthur.

"Me too," says a voice from the back.

"Hear, hear," says another.

"Sounds like a statement your lawyer instructed you to make," says Benjamin.

"I might want to work with you on the paper," says another voice from the back.

"I work part-time for a travel agency, and I can help you get a better deal on your next spur-of-the-moment trip," says Jim.

Alice turns to Josie and quietly says, "I think what Rodney said was acceptable as an apology, but I'm not sure. I think it was a little too slick."

Josie says to her, not quite as quietly, "Well, he had the good sense to leave Texas. I'll give him that."

Have I got a topic for you!

"You probably know by now that Newt Gingrich's petition to be on the Virginia ballot has also been turned down," says Rennie as he begins the next class.

"For those who missed last week's class, our meeting was a bit disrupted by the news that Texas governor Rick Perry has failed to get on the Virginia ballot.

"We may have had a few broken toes, but I understand those usually heal quickly. We certainly experienced a cacophony of voices, cell phone rings, and some non-academic language not usually heard in a classroom."

Josie leans over to Bill. "Oh yeah? I wonder where *he* went to school."

Rennie looks in her direction. "Josie, could I see you for a minute after class?"

He then refocuses on the whole class. "We've concentrated so far on who's allowed to vote and how people get to be candidates. Next week, we'll be talking about some other problematic aspects of elections.

"And I don't need to remind you that your term paper is due in six weeks…"

The teachers groan.

"And, you remember, don't you, that in addition to the written paper, you'll also be giving the class a talk of twenty to thirty minutes on your chosen topic?"

More groans.

"Don't forget that you must have your topic approved in advance.

"Any questions?"

Silence.

Dusty pipes up, "I'd like to ask the second question now."

Mostly puzzled looks.

"That's my boy. I'm glad someone's learned something here," Rennie laughs. "Dusty was referring to a line I used three weeks ago. Good memory!"

Dusty nods. Rennie smiles, then continues on.

"I have a few suggestions for term papers if you're having trouble getting started." He walks around the room handing out lists of his suggestions to those with their hand raised. "And we can end early today. I'll stick around if anybody would like to talk with me about their project now."

A general rush for the door. Josie stays behind and approaches Rennie.

"You wanted to see me?"

"Yes, I did. Are you free for dinner tonight?"

She pauses a moment. "I'd love to, but I have a term paper to work on."

Topics and Tropics

A group of teachers sit in a restaurant and discuss the term paper assignment. Their large round table is cluttered with papers, books, and menus.

Benjamin intently scans the list of possible topics that Rennie handed him in class. "I wouldn't know how to find the answer to any of these questions on the internet."

"When I started teaching, the internet wasn't even a twinkle in anyone's eye," notes Jim.

"He's asking us to think!" says Benjamin, shaking his head so fiercely that his baseball cap falls off. "If we tried pulling something like this on *our* students we'd be fired!"

"Well, not quite," says Emily. "When I first began teaching I tried to get students to think, and I only got a warning letter in my file."

"That reminds me," says Dusty. "A school system I once worked in tried to get me to develop a two-stage program in creativity. I read the specs carefully. They called for a two-stage process: first to identify it, then to stamp it out. Of course I declined.

"I got a warning letter in *my* file for that one." Dusty takes a look at his list. "Hey, look at this topic Rennie suggested:

Critically compare how two countries with free elections, the United States and another country from a different continent, decide who gets to be on the ballot."

"You lived in Canada for a while, didn't you, Jim?" asks Benjamin.

"Well, I, uh, yes. A long, long time ago. I was stationed in Toronto during the Vietnam War."

"*Stationed in Toronto*? You mean you were a *draft dodger*?" asks Gregory.

"No. A *war resister*."

More puzzled looks. Some edge their chairs away from Jim.

"Is that, like, a deserter?" asks Gregory.

"Would that be a problem for you if it was?" answers Jim.

An uncomfortable silence as Gregory thinks it over.

"Would anyone like to share the Greek salad with me?" asks Alice.

"I lived in Mexico for a year, but I don't know anything about the political system there," says Gregory.

"You couldn't use that anyway. It's not on a different continent," says Dusty.

"It's not?" says Gregory. "It seemed like it was."

A try-out for Emily and Bill

Emily and Bill are in Rennie's office, seated across the desk from him.

Bill begins, "We'd like to discuss a term paper topic that's not on your list."

Emily continues, "It's like, the topics on your list are so…yesterday."

Rennie looks puzzled. "Yesterday?" He glances at his wall calendar.

Emily backtracks, "Well, so twentieth century."

"Here's our idea," says Bill. He looks down at some notes in his lap. "In our classrooms, we've been experimenting with something inspired by what you said about how teachers select their class reps."

Emily looks up from her own notes. "And we think we can apply what we've learned to a brand new way to select our Representatives in Congress."

"Something *I* said?"

Bill breaks in. "Well, not in so many words. But you got us thinking about how a teacher who gives each kid an equal chance to be the rep is *really* giving a positive lesson in democracy."

"But," adds Emily, "it could be a *negative* lesson if a teacher chooses the class trouble-maker just to get the kid out of the classroom."

"Okay, I see," says Rennie.

He smiles broadly and looks at Emily. "What approach do *you* take?"

Bill shoves his notes into his jacket pocket.

"Well, both Emily and I teach first grade, and we don't have class reps at that level. The private school I teach in has just twelve first-graders. And each one of those twelve *loves* to be the monitor for the dry-erase board.

"Maybe you remember feeling the same way as a first-grader, Rennie?"

"Actually, I don't remember what 'dry-erase' is."

"Might be a generational thing," says Emily. "Think 'chalkboard.'"

Rennie looks even more confused.

"Let's back it up again," says Bill. "How about 'blackboard'?"

"Bingo!" says Rennie.

Bill goes on. "So, every twelve school days, I draw all the students' names from cards in a fishbowl. I then list them, in the order their names came up, on a calendar I post that shows the date for each student's turn as Dry-Erase Monitor."

"And that works pretty well?"

"Yes," says Bill. "Except the time I pulled out a guppy."

Emily giggles. That wasn't in her script. Rennie laughs long and loud. Bill smiles.

Rennie reaches into a desk cabinet and pulls out a bottle of wine and three glasses. He pours. Bill and Emily exchange glances, shrug, and each accept a glass.

Rennie turns to Emily.

"And you choose your Dry-Erase Monitors the same way?"

"No, my class has thirty-five students. Bill's system wouldn't work for me.

"My first-graders at the bottom of the list would be too twitchy to wait for their turn. So I put each child's name on a separate card. I shuffle the cards each morning, then draw the name of that day's lucky student. That sparks everyone's interest. And helps wake up the sleepy ones."

"And that works pretty well for you? No guppies in the ointment, so to speak?"

"Nope. My approach instantly gets the class involved every morning. But recently…"

Her voice fades out and a tear trickles down her cheek.

Bill puts one arm around her and reaches to hold her hand.

"But recently?" prompts Rennie.

"Well, my principal has been receiving complaints from a parent…" Emily stops to wipe her eyes. "A parent who's been in Gamblers Anonymous for seven years."

Rennie looks puzzled, starts to laugh, then smoothly segues it into a cough. He takes a big gulp of his wine, and refreshes Emily's glass.

"What was it you guys came to see me about today exactly?"

"The topic for our term paper," says Bill. "Think of a hypothetical huge fishbowl that contains the names of each adult citizen in an election district on a separate card. "Then, instead of holding an election, every two years a card is chosen at random from the bowl, and the person named on it becomes that district's Representative in Congress."

"That's the model," adds Emily, who has regained her composure. "Of course, a computerized list would actually be used, not a fishbowl.

"What do you think?"

"Well," says Rennie, "nobody could accuse you of tweaking the system. Destroying it, perhaps."

He looks down at his empty glass, and squares his shoulders.

"Your idea has originality, pitfalls, advantages, disadvantages, and also unknown consequences. You can definitely expect very angry reactions, and not just from Gamblers Anonymous." He pauses. "I love it."

Emily and Bill hug each other. Then, to celebrate the success of their meeting, Bill refills Rennie's glass.

Rennie looks thoughtful. "It will take a lot of work. Very ambitious for a term paper. Come see me next week and we'll discuss how to make it a manageable project for just two people."

He pauses again. "Actually, I think it would be better with three. Bring Josie."

"Well," says Bill, "it might be better if we didn't."

"But we'll bring…the bottle," adds Emily.

"Actually," says Rennie, "it might be better if you didn't. I'm trying to cut back."

Emily smiles. "We may just come empty-handed then."

"You'll both still be very welcome," says Rennie.

The Emily and Bill Show on Prime Time

Rennie stands in front of the class. Bill and Emily are seated behind him, just in front of a projection screen.

"We have discussed many problems with the election system," begins Rennie.

"*You've* discussed, we've *listened*," whispers Josie.

"Now, in the class's first oral report, Emily and Bill will present their proposal for a change in how we select our House of Representatives that gets around some of these problems.

"Is that a fair statement?" he asks, as he looks behind him at Emily and Bill.

The three of them smile at each other. Emily and Bill step forward, and Rennie takes Bill's vacated seat.

"Actually, our proposal could get rid of *all* these problems," says Bill.

The audience leans forward.

"Feel free at any time to interrupt us to ask any question…," says Bill.

"…that we know the answer to," adds Emily.

Some chuckles from the audience. Bill and Emily high five each other.

Bill clicks on a hand-held device. "This slide shows our idea in just two sentences." Bill points to the screen:

An enormous fishbowl contains the name of every adult citizen in a particular election district on separate slips of paper.

Every two years, a slip of paper is chosen at random from the bowl, and the person named on that slip becomes the district's Representative in Congress.

"That's the model," says Emily. "Of course, we would actually use a computerized list, not a fishbowl.

"This new system has many advantages.

"With *elections*, rich people and corporations can 'buy' Representatives by giving large contributions to their election campaigns, and sometimes to the campaigns of their major party opponents too. Then the Representatives they've bought will vote the way their 'owners' want, in order to gain financial support for their next campaign.

"But with a *lottery*, a prospective owner won't know in advance whom to buy among the thousands of names in that fishbowl."

"But Emily," says Alice, "what about *post-lottery* bribes to the winners?"

Emily pauses a moment.

"Well, I don't think we can *eliminate* bribery by using a lottery to choose our Representatives," she says. "But, Alice, we can make it *less likely*.

"With an election, the briber knows who the candidates are, and can use information about the stands they took on various issues during the election campaign. And, if a candidate has previously held office, about how they voted in the past. So the briber knows which candidate may be more favorable to his or her cause, and can approach that person sooner."

"With either an election *or* a lottery," says Alice, "the briber could promise the winning Representative a high-pay-for-no-work job or consulting fees, or even a place on the Board of Directors of an organization.

"Of course, a *lottery* winner is highly unlikely to win office again. So the bribing community would vigorously oppose a switch from elections to lotteries."

"Well, I think you're right about that," says Emily.

"I have to admit your phrase 'the bribing community' makes me chuckle, Alice," says Rennie.

"W-well, you told us early on that humor was permitted."

"Touché," says Rennie. "But aren't we being a little paranoid here?"

"Maybe," says Alice, "but why do so many school systems have written policies against us teachers accepting Christmas gifts from the parents of kids in our classes?

"I think often these gifts are intended as bribes for us to give their kids extra help, overlook their bad behavior, and, in the upper grades, to get us to write glowing letters of recommendation for them."

"I think you're right," says Emily. "I had assumed that the reps chosen by lottery would, in general, have more integrity. But I do always wonder about the motives of those who actively seek to become candidates and win an election."

"Well, *you* may be right," says Alice. "Anyway, I'm glad I didn't violate your rule by asking something you didn't have an answer to."

"Well, actually, you did," says Emily. "It's just that I think fast on my feet."

"Well, that's a good quality to have. And thank you for your willingness and ability to enliven this class," replies Alice.

Some scattered applause.

From the back of the room, Arthur's resonant voice is heard.

"You just told us that under the lottery system it's most unlikely that reps will serve a second term, and you paint that as an advantage.

"But doesn't it also mean that after their reps one term in office, an election district would *lose* his or her experience and knowledge of how to get things done in Washington?

"The short answer, Arthur, is no," says Emily. "Again, I'm making some assumptions here, and you might make different ones.

"I've been watching the televised debates of the Republican Party candidates leading up to the Presidential Primaries. Most of the debaters have already been elected and re-elected to such positions as Governor, Representative, and Senator. And there's also the occasional womanizer and an owner of a chain of pizza parlors.

"Have you been watching, too?"

"Well, a little bit…just at halftime…depends on the entertainment," says Arthur.

Emily replies, "I haven't been impressed by their platforms, or thinking ability. And most of all, their ability to get things done in Washington, the same ability most of them accuse all the others of not having. So I don't see reps serving just one term as a disadvantage of the lottery system."

Emily mops her forehead. "Bill, could you step up and discuss the next advantage?"

Bill comes forward and stands with Emily in front of the class, facing them.

"To continue our comparison of elections and lotteries, let's consider *simplicity*," he says.

"Here's the situation: Rep. Gabrielle Giffords (D-Ariz.) announces she will resign from Congress while she recovers from being shot in the head by a constituent. A replacement must be found for her.

"And here's what the *election* procedure will be," says Bill.

"According to state law, Gov. Jan Brewer (R-Ariz.) must set a date for a special election primary 80 to 90 days after Giffords formally steps down, and a general election will be set for 50 to 60 days after the primary. So the primary election for Giffords' seat will likely be held in late April with the general election in June. *Washington Post, Jan. 22, 2012"*

"The *lottery* procedure," says Bill, "would mean just taking another dip into the fishbowl."

"The lottery's definitely simpler," says Alice.

"And cheaper," adds Arthur.

"And we can throw out the primary," says Dusty. "Who needs it?"

"Wait just a minute there," says Benjamin. "You can't just suddenly make a change like that. I mean, we've had primary elections for hundreds, maybe thousands of years. It's the American way of doing things."

"Are you saying that everything we do now we should always continue to do?" asks Bill.

"Well, yeah!" says Benjamin.

Bill rolls his eyes.

"Do you also believe that nothing should ever be done for the first time?" asks Emily.

In the next-to-last row, a male student whispers into the ear of the student sitting next to him. She slaps his hand.

"Yeah," says Benjamin. "Well, that's a little tricky. When you have this new thing you want to do, you have to ask whether the Constitution will allow it."

"Suppose the Constitution itself doesn't say anything about it, but one of the Amendments says you can do it," says Emily. "Could you do it then?"

"Those Amendments. You've hit a sore spot there," says Benjamin. "Some of them are all right, I guess, but some…You've got to ask yourself what the Founding Fathers were smoking, you know what I mean?"

"What about the *First* Amendment? Is it okay?" asks Emily.

"Uh, the first?" asks Benjamin.

"Yes," says Emily. "The one that talks about freedom of speech, freedom of the press, freedom of religion, stuff like that."

"Yeah, that was all good stuff," says Benjamin. "But when you go beyond that…I mean, you get to the point where…Well, if you've got a basically good document like the Constitution, then stick with it. Don't mess it up."

"In general," says Emily, "before the Civil War, the North was against slavery, and the South favored it. It was the 13th Amendment in 1865 that prohibited slavery."

"Yeah, I know just what you mean," says Benjamin. "Back in 1973, the Major Leagues took different stands on an issue. The American League permitted designated hitters, and the National League didn't. Baseball hasn't been the same since."

Bill turns away and puts both hands over his face to hide his giggle.

"Well, we could get into this as deeply as you want," says Benjamin. "I enjoy it. I teach American History. But when you start mixing history and politics and God only knows what else, you don't know what you're going to get. It's a real crap shoot."

"Thanks for sharing your views with us," says Emily.

Bill, no longer able to contain his laughter, heads quickly for the door.

"Let's take a ten-minute break, and then Bill will lead the discussion," says Emily.

Dusty and Emily both rush toward Alice from

different sides. Dusty arrives a step sooner.

Alice smiles at Dusty. "Could you give us a couple of minutes for some girl chat?"

Dusty smiles and leaves. Emily hugs Alice.

Girl Chat

Emily puts down her coffee cup. "You made some strong points in there, and very effectively too."

"Thanks. But I'm still terrified about giving my term project report."

"You'll be fine, Alice. Tell me, is this something new, you and Dusty?"

Alice blushes. "Well, we've seen each other a couple of times."

"Seen each other?"

"You know, coffee, a walk, sometimes a snack after class."

"So how's it going?"

"Well, we've reached some understandings."

"Like?"

"He won't talk about baseball, and I won't go on and on about how insecure I feel."

Emily laughs.

"Sounds promising," she says. Alice nods. Then she too laughs.

They stand up, hug, and slowly head back to class.

The attack of the Killer App

Ten minutes later, not one student has returned. After twenty minutes, about half of them have come back. Bill begins speaking.

"We've seen that selecting the House of Representatives by lottery has the advantages of simplicity, economy, and speed," says Bill.

Most of the missing students hurry back in.

"But have I made a sale?" asks Bill. "Do you buy this new approach?"

"I work evenings selling computers and electronic gadgets," says Arthur, "and some of it is really neat stuff.

"But it doesn't move off the shelf unless I can demonstrate that it offers some new feature that people think they just must have. What we call the 'killer app.' It's short for killer application.

"So what would be the killer app for your lottery system?" asks Arthur.

"Emily and I have been talking about this with each other," says Bill, "although we've never used that term. Because we've never heard of it."

"To us," says Emily, "holding elections is one way to choose our representatives, but it's not the best way. It's cumbersome, expensive, and open to abuse.

"And who we wind up with can't truly represent us because, quite frankly, they aren't *like* us. I think what I'm going to say next will especially strike home to a large group of people here."

Emily has their attention.

"Right now, in 2012, how many members of the House of Representatives are women? Any guesses?"

Some whispering and muttering, but nobody offers a guess.

Finally, Emily says, "Seventy-six of the 435, or a little over 17%."

Louder muttering, especially from the women.

"If we had used a national lottery to select the current House of Representatives, what percentage of the members would be women?" asks Emily.

"Fifty percent," says Josie.

"Actually about 52%, the percentage of the population over 18 that is female," says Millicent Albright, who has quietly entered the room unnoticed.

"I'm sorry to break in like this, Rennie," she continues, "but the Dean must see you right away."

Rennie, startled, takes a deep breath. Then he turns to Dusty and says, "Would you take notes for me while I'm gone?" He looks over at Emily, smiles and gives her a "thumbs-up" signal. She smiles back uncertainly.

Millicent takes Rennie's arm and walks out with him.

Face Time with the Dean

Millicent knocks on the door to the Dean's office and quickly ushers Rennie in before receiving a response.

The Dean nods at Rennie and he points to a chair for him in front of his over-sized desk. Rennie sits down. Millicent pulls over another chair for herself, ignoring the hostile stares of the Dean.

Rennie looks directly at the Dean. "I have no idea what you're going to say, but I'd like Millicent to hear it too. It may affect her."

The Dean ignores Millicent. "I've held off giving the University's Board of Trustees copies of a letter I've received, because it will reflect badly on you. I've known you a long time, Rennie, and I thought that it would be only fair to hear your side first."

"Coincidentally, Gerald," says Rennie, with traces of a grin on his face, "*I've* known *you* a long time too. Would it be too much for me to ask to see this letter before I comment further?"

"Not at all," says Gerald, reaching for a folder on his desktop. "You've always had a very keen mind, Rennie. You were the very first person I thought of when Professor Leonard's sudden death created an urgent and unexpected teaching vacancy for us. Here's the letter."

Rennie reaches out with one hand for the single sheet of paper, and with his other hand waves Millicent over to read the letter with him.

It doesn't take long to read.

Dear Ms. Kunstler:

I was shocked to learn from my son, a pupil in your first-grade class, that you are encouraging gambling behavior among the youngsters in your care by the way in which you choose each morning who will be that day's Dry-Erase Monitor.

As a member of Gamblers Anonymous for seven lucky years, I am appalled at your behavior, and unless it ceases immediately, I will report you to the proper authorities.

Best wishes for the holiday season.

Rennie puts the paper onto the desk in front of him. "How did this unsigned, undated letter, apparently addressed to my student Emily Kunstler, happen to come into your hands, Gerald?" he asks. "When did you get it? And what have you done since you received it?"

The Dean takes out and lights a cigar. Millicent hurriedly returns to her seat, which she then drags even further away from the lit cigar.

"The parent also sent a copy of the letter to Ms. Kunstler's school principal," says Gerald. "In talking with Ms. Kunstler, the principal discovered that she was a student in your class, what's it called again? *SCRATCHING A COUNTRY: Destroying the United States of America?*

Did I get that right?" he asks.

"Well, something like that," says Rennie.

The Dean takes a puff on his cigar. As the smoke reaches her, Millie gets up and rushes out of the office.

"I'm trying to understand the somewhat twisted logic here," continues Rennie. "Emily, a student in my course, *Starting a Country from Scratch: Re-Forming the United States of America*, has developed and now uses innovative techniques as a first-grade teacher in a public school not affiliated with this university. And you believe this could reflect badly on *me*?"

Rennie pauses and thinks, *And would reflect, even more badly, on you for hiring me.*

"You've got to understand, Rennie. We're all living under the shadow of those nasty events at Penn State," says Gerald. "Have you forgotten already? The President of the University forced to resign. The Associate Football Coach fired, indicted, and convicted on 45 counts of sexual abuse. The students portrayed on national TV as rioters. The school's reputation shattered. The football program in shambles. The coach, once a national hero, forced to resign, and dead a few months later."

"Hold on there," says Rennie. "You connect all this to a letter someone wrote to Emily's principal, a letter I hadn't seen until a few minutes ago, and you say you're shielding *me* from *my* looking bad if this letter is released to the University's Board of Trustees?"

"Rennie, these are difficult times for all of us. When we first talked about your teaching this course, I had hoped that it could get you back on to a tenure track at our honorable university.

"Can you help to bring satisfactory closure to this unfortunate situation? That would give me a powerful weapon in my struggle to get you back into academia where you belong."

"I'm not so sure I want to come back," says Rennie.

"Don't you have a dream?" asks Gerald.

Rennie closes his eyes for a moment but no dream comes to him. Finally, he says, "I'd like to develop another new course, *Field Work in Alternative Political Organizing*. But academia no longer holds the appeal for me it once did."

"Perhaps something related, Rennie, where you could put your valuable skills to good use. A foundation job? A position at a well-paying nonprofit think-tank? Some dream you've put on the back-burner, for which I could put in a good word to help bring it forward again?

"If you could speak to Emily, her principal, and the parent, and have everyone agree to a solution that makes clear that neither this University nor Emily's principal, nor Emily herself for that matter, condones any act that might give the impression that making gambling attractive to first-graders is okay, then I would be extremely grateful to you. I'd go out of my way to help you advance in your professional career. You'll just have to let me know what career that would be."

Rennie remembers the last general faculty meeting the Dean organized the Super Bowl Total Point

Prediction Lottery ("SuBoToPoPreLo"), and coerced 100% faculty participation.

"A certain percentage of all funds collected will go to a deserving senior who otherwise would be unable to attend our graduate school. Don't be the last member of your department to purchase lottery tickets. Only a few are left. The average purchase per faculty member in your department has been for $625".

Rennie will not bring that up now. *Gerald focuses on a hypothetical "deserving senior," and meanwhile Millie hasn't gotten a raise in three years.*

He says. "I'll think it over. I know you like to move quickly." *He recalls the day a year ago when the Dean fired him a few hours after finding out that Rennie had allowed students to decide their own course grades.*

The Dean winces.

"I'll get back to you about this tomorrow morning at ten," says Rennie.

The Next Morning

The Dean offers Rennie a warm handshake. Rennie smiles, declines a cigar, but accepts a cup of coffee.

"I've got some good news for you," says Rennie.

The return of the Killer App

"I'll accept the 52% estimate from Millicent at the Registrar's Office," says Emily. "If there's one thing they know how to do there, it's count.

"But the difference between the 17% we *have* and the 52% we *could and should have* is enormous. If as a group women feel strongly about an issue, like federal funding for abortion, and men feel differently about it, then women now find it almost impossible to prevail.

"I've chosen gender in my example because it's an important category, where the make-up of the House of Representatives is dramatically different from that of the general population. But I might have chosen such things as financial status, age, sexual orientation, native-born vs. naturalized immigrant, and first language spoken to make the same point.

"And in each case, we would find the make-up of Congress to be very different from the make-up of the people they are supposed to represent.

"For example, a recent incoming 'freshman class' of Congress showed that the 94 new Representatives had a median net worth of about $1,067,000. The typical American household had about $1 million less.

"The simplest way to insure that Congress and the people they are supposed to represent are similar in all these variables is to choose Congress by a lottery or some other random method.

"And, ladies and gentlemen," Emily concludes, "there's your killer app for the lottery system."

A path toward world peace?

"Well done, Emily," says Arthur. "You too, Bill.

"Emily, when you implied that Benjamin believes that 'nothing should ever be done for the first time,' and that 'nothing we now do should ever be discontinued,' you may not have known that some of us in the business world are more enlightened in these matters.

"*We* would say, 'nothing should ever be done for the first time unless we can make money doing it and not get caught,' and 'nothing we now do should ever be discontinued unless we can sneak it past those damned unions.'"

"If we switched to this new lottery system, how would the political parties we now have be affected?" asks Gregory.

"All the Representatives would be free to join and resign from any existing party, form a new party, and join or withdraw from informal alliances with any other representatives, whenever they chose," says Emily.

"The switch-over to the lottery system might first occur in just one progressive state. If so, I'm betting on California. But it could also be in any of the 50 states."

"If it's just one state, I'm betting on Colorado," says a smoker's voice from the back of the room.

"Your use of the word 'betting' made me think of Nevada," says a female voice from the back, "where gambling in all forms is so much a part of the culture. I'd put my money on Nevada to be the first state to flip."

"Would this be the end of those annoying political parties we now have?" asks Josie.

"I hope so," says Bill.

"I wonder if we could really have a situation with *elections* for the members of the House of Representatives in some states, and *lotteries* to choose them in others," says Alice.

"Well," says Emily, "Rennie has told us that the Constitution leaves out the details of how the states should select their representatives. Ultimately, the Supreme Court may have to decide if using a lottery is a valid 'election' procedure. As I've pointed out, it has some unique advantages."

"Suppose one cohort of representatives chosen by lottery involves the country in a war and a later cohort votes not to support that war. Could we abruptly cease fighting?" asks Jim.

"Yes," says Bill. "At the least, the later cohort could get one year added to its term in office as a bonus for outstanding performance."

"But that would mean…" Gregory starts to say.

"Well, there are many paths to world peace," says Bill. "This may be one of them."

Race

"Emily, you didn't mention race when you talked about groups that may not be adequately represented in Congress," says Arthur. "Why?"

"Well, we use the term 'race' to refer to similarities and differences we notice among people in their physical appearance," says Emily. "Scientists today tend to avoid this term. They do not find these differences to be consistently related to anything else that's important."

"They don't?" Arthur obviously can't believe what he's hearing. "But it's just common sense."

"Common sense tells us the world is flat and the sun revolves around the earth," Emily says.

Gregory appears very agitated. He thinks, *'Common sense' is sort of like 'relative democracy'! It can mean different things to different people. No wonder my ESL students have trouble with English.*

This line of argument intrigues some teachers, others can't follow it. In their heads, still others develop plans to picket against the ideas they have just met.

The Big Two: Fit in or get out

The first two rows of the lecture hall are filled with teachers wearing t-shirts that say on the front,

Keep Elections!
Let the People Choose!

and on the back,

RACE IS
IMPORTANT

Row three is empty.

Most of those seated in row four, and a scattered few seated in the remaining rows, wear t-shirts that say on the front,

We want our reps
to look like us.
GO LOTTERY!

and on the back,

I WON'T VOTE ANYMORE!

Rennie stands in front of the room and faces the class. *His* t-shirt message, if any, is obscured by his long-sleeved cotton shirt and sports jacket.

"Good afternoon," he says. "I'm sorry I was summoned away by the Dean last week and couldn't get back here while our class was still in session. I understand it ended on a somewhat discordant note, and that the discord spilled out on to the streets the next day.

"I'm glad the term 'killer app' remained just a metaphor.

"I don't know what you've learned this past week. From looking around I see two distinct groups here that I'll call 'pro-election' and 'pro-lottery.' We can easily see who's who by the t-shirt they wear.

"I'm wondering two things," says Rennie. "First, to all the t-shirt wearers, where did you get the time and money to get those t-shirts made?"

"I'll address that, Rennie," says Dusty, proudly sporting a 'Go Lottery' t-shirt. "On Friday afternoons, schools empty early, and those of us who are activists come out to play at what's meaningful to us.

"Some of us don't have much money. So we try to guilt family members and friends into making a contribution, and when needed, we kick in what we can afford ourselves," he says.

"It's funny," says Arthur, a wearer of a 'Keep Elections' t-shirt. "We espouse an opposite point of view, but use the same tactics.

"What was the second thing you were wondering about, Rennie?"

"Most people here don't display *any* t-shirt message," says Rennie.

"Maybe you're not sure about the best way to choose our representatives in Congress.

"Or maybe you don't want to make your opinion public now. I don't want you to feel like no-message-bearing outcasts! To stay with the t-shirt theme I'll just call you…the 'Wash Warm, Tumble Dry' group.

"And then again, you may have a strong opinion that you're perfectly willing to share, but none of the available t-shirts go with your outfit."

Some tittering in the class at that last remark.

"And some, as Dusty and Arthur just told us, don't have the time, money, or perhaps even the inclination," says Rennie. "I'm surprised how strongly some of you, on both sides, feel about this issue."

"You've brought it out in us," says Josie.

Rennie smiles. "People are complicated, and labels over-simplify," he says. "You may be in the pro-election group and still see merit in the pro-lottery position, or vice versa.

"You may be a 'Wash Warmer,' but not a 'Tumble Dryer.'"

"And whatever group you're in, you may have questions to ask about the presentations you've heard so far, and about those you'll hear later on."

"For the next twenty minutes. I'd like those who are pro-election to meet here on my right, and those who are pro-lottery to meet there on my left.

"Decide on three questions you want your group to present to the rest of the class, and also decide who in your group will present them.

"We'll *all* reconvene here promptly in twenty minutes. Any questions before we begin?"

"Like you said before, most of us don't have a t-shirt message. What do *we* do?" asks Alice.

"If you don't feel comfortable in either group, you can go for coffee," says Rennie. "The place across the street makes a decent cup. I don't recommend their pastry, though."

"You mean we don't have to stick around?" asks Arthur.

"I expect you back in twenty minutes, Arthur," replies Rennie. "All of you."

"Does the same person in a group ask all of that group's three questions?"

"It's up to the group, Bill," says Rennie.

"I'm not pro-election or pro-lottery. How do *I* get to ask a question?" asks Dusty.

"You just did," says Rennie.

"But you didn't give me a real answer," says Dusty.

"Good point," says Rennie.

"You still haven't!"

"Another good point. Look, the system isn't *designed* to give you an answer."

"What system? And what *is* it designed to do?" asks Dusty.

"The Two-Party System. It's designed to keep all the power within the two major parties. Which aren't really that different from each other," says Rennie.

"So because I don't belong to either party, I can't ask these parties a question today?"

"I wouldn't say you can't, I'd say it's difficult."

"What would I have to do?" asks Dusty.

"Get me signatures from twenty-five of your classmates on a petition requesting you, a non-member of either party, be allowed to ask a question today when we reconvene, and I'd be inclined to look favorably upon it."

"Are you kidding? In just twenty minutes, I'm to get signatures on a petition I haven't written yet from twenty-five classmates who are busy at a meeting or drinking coffee across the street?"

"Well," says Rennie, "those attending the meetings aren't eligible to sign *your* petition anyway. They've already shown commitment to one of the two major parties. Only uncommitted citizens can sign a petition on your behalf."

Dusty struggles to contain his frustration.

"And actually, you have just seventeen minutes now," says Rennie.

Dusty clenches his fists. He's losing his struggle.

"And yes," says Rennie, smiling. "I have been kidding. Sometimes my peculiar sense of humor helps me get a point across. I hope my unorthodox approach didn't upset you, Dusty."

"I… No, your approach didn't upset me. Well, a bit. I'll get over it."

He begins to relax one fist.

"But you weren't kidding about the system, were you?"

"No."

"Oh my God!" says Dusty.

He slowly relaxes his other fist.

"I wanted to prepare you," says Rennie, "for what you'll experience if you take the next course in this series, *Field Work in Alternative Political Organizing*.

"Okay, time to saddle up, everybody. Your twenty minutes start for real now."

Some students leave right away. About a dozen students go to each location Rennie has indicated.

In the pro-election group, two or three people do almost all the talking. After a few minutes, the others leave in disgust.

In the pro-lottery group, most stay fifteen minutes before the group breaks up.

Rennie wanders around the room, glancing here and there, listening.

Dusty sees a chance to talk to him alone. He approaches.

"Rennie, I'm feeling a lot better now, and I understand your teaching methods better, too. Could I ask you just one more question?"

Rennie smiles. "Of course."

"What did the Dean want to talk to you about last week?"

Rennie hesitates a moment. "Could you hold off a while about this, Dusty? I'd like to tell the class about it all at the same time."

Dusty hesitates a moment, then smiles.

"Sure," he replies. "You're the boss."

When most students have returned, Rennie holds up a coin.

"This is for which group gets to ask the first question. Heads, pro-election group, tails, pro-lottery group," he says.

He flips the coin.

"Heads. Okay, who will start for the pro-election group?"

"I will. I'm Jerry, and I'd like to know…"

"Hold your question just a minute, Jerry," says Rennie. "How did your group pick you to start? Did you hold an election?"

"Well, uh, no. I volunteered. No one else wanted to."

"And how did your group choose the three questions you want to ask the pro-lottery group?"

"We all tossed out ideas for questions and someone wrote them down."

"Then you voted to determine the top three?"

"Well, we never got around to it. Everybody left, so I picked out my three favorites."

"Okay," says Rennie. "And who will answer for the pro-lottery group?"

"Me. I'm Sherrie, and I was chosen by lottery."

"Okay, Sherrie, thanks. So what I've heard here," says Rennie, "is that each group believes in a different method, and the pro-lottery group believes strongly enough to actually use theirs."

Trust

Rennie arrives at the lecture hall and sees Dusty waiting for him just outside. Rennie puts his arm around Dusty's shoulders, and they enter together.

Rennie immediately spots Emily and rushes over to her. He leads her to the back of the room, where they engage in a soft but animated discussion.

The rest of the class continues its noisy chatter, until Josie comes to the front of the room, puts her forefinger on her lips, and says, "Shush, everybody. Let's try to hear what they're saying."

Rennie and Emily notice the reduction in the general sound level. Emily is heard saying, "I trust you." They quickly conclude their conversation. Then they hug each other and separate. Emily goes to her usual seat, and Rennie to the front of the room.

"I was summoned to the Dean's office last week during our class meeting," says Rennie. "When I got back here, the class hour had already ended. I'd like to tell you now what it was all about.

"Basically it's about Emily, but in a larger sense, it concerns all of us. Emily has graciously agreed for her and I to share some information with you, but on the condition that what we say here today does not go out of this room.

"If you don't agree to that condition, please leave now."

Nobody moves.

Dusty shouts out, "What happens in Indiana stays in Indiana." The class laughs and applauds. Rennie joins in.

"Now here's what happened when I met the Dean. He informed me that Emily had received an unsigned letter from a parent whose son is in Emily's first grade class. The letter writer complained that Emily was encouraging gambling behavior in her class by the way in which she chose each day's Dry-Erase Monitor. The writer said that he or she is a member of *Gamblers Anonymous*.

"I had thought that the writer might be from *Informants Anonymous*.

"Just a few minutes ago, Emily told me that her classroom techniques are now being questioned by a member of a different organization. Let's hear about that directly from Emily."

Emily comes forward. "Thanks, Rennie," she says.

"I have only so much instructional time in the day," she begins. "When I use the lottery to choose the dry-erase monitor, I'm teaching fairness and openness in decision-making, and it's fun for the kids. And I enjoy it too. It takes about two minutes.

"So, I asked myself where this time could come from.

"And what is the instructional value of the Pledge of Allegiance, anyhow?

"Something had to go. My choice enraged an anonymous parent who claimed to be a member of the American Legion. Maybe it's the same parent; both letters were unsigned."

A voice from the back calls out, "You're one gutsy teacher."

An enraged voice from the next seat shouts, "This woman is a danger to our country."

The two teachers glare at each other.

Rennie steps in. "As I expected, there are different opinions about Emily's teaching decision. I'd like to gather your opinions more systematically through an election, rather than a shout-out procedure. This will also let us observe the nitty-gritty problems that can come up in casting a vote.

"I'm going to hand out a blank piece of paper to each of you. Use it as a 'ballot' to vote on how you think Emily should spend her two minutes.

"If you think she should use a lottery system to choose the Dry-Erase Monitor, write the letters DEM on your paper ballot.

"If you think she should lead the class in reciting the Pledge of Allegiance, write the letters PoA. Don't use a capital 'o' or your ballot will be disqualified.

"I'll come around very shortly to collect these ballots," Rennie says.

"A question," says Alice. "In rushing, I just made my 'o' a little too large, so it might *appear* to be a capital, which is *not* what I intended. What can I..."

"Sorry, ma'am, I'll have to disqualify your vote," says Rennie. "This is a *secret* ballot, and you've just disclosed *your* voting preference to a roomful of voters. Furthermore, you did it within ten feet of the voting area, the fine for which could be as much as $500 and a week of jail time."

Rennie sees that Alice looks quite distraught. "Relax, Alice," he says. "Remember when we went over the class outline I promised there would be some role-playing exercises? Well, this is one of them." He smiles at her.

"I get it now," says Alice. She smiles briefly, then her face hardens. "If you disqualify my vote, you're going straight to hell!"

Rennie moves on quickly to pick up the next ballot.

A few voters later, he stops in front of Arthur. "Sir, I don't remember seeing you before around town. Are you new here?"

"I've been living in Tokyo the past year," says Arthur. "Just got back last night." He looks at his watch. "Between the jet lag and the time change…"

"Do you have local ID?"

"I've got my U.S. passport right here."

"This is a local election, sir," says Rennie. "I'll put your ballot in the pile of those that the Election Board will look over *only* if the tally of verified ballots shows that the questionable ones, like yours, might make a difference in the final results."

He moves on to the next row. Things go smoothly until he reaches Josie. In a quick glance at her ballot, he reads, *I'm free for dinner tonight.* He is startled and hopes it doesn't show. He is also excited.

He looks down at Josie's "ballot" and says loudly, "How did my shopping list wind up here?" He pockets the "ballot" to laughter and applause.

He then rushes through the remaining rows collecting ballots, and returns to the front of the room. He asks Emily to assist him in tallying the votes.

A few minutes later, Emily reports back to Rennie, who in turn tells the class:

"The Dry-Erase Monitor, 23 votes. The Pledge of Allegiance, 22 votes."

An outbreak of cheers, jeers, and shouts.

"Hold it," says Rennie, "there's more.

"Since the DEM's and PoA's differ by only one vote, two questionable votes will be forwarded to the Election Board for a decision as to their legitimacy."

Another outbreak of cheers, jeers, and shouts. Rennie glances down at his watch.

"Hold it a minute, please," says Rennie, "there's still more. Frankly, I didn't anticipate all this."

He looks in the general direction of Benjamin and Dusty. "There were two write-in votes. Identically worded: 'Have the class spend the time singing, *Take me out to the ballgame*.'"

Slowly, a very excited, talkative group of students leaves the room. Only one remains.

Rennie walks over to the remaining one, pulls out the piece of paper that he had earlier called his shopping list, and returns it to Josie with a wink.

Couples

Later that evening, Josie and Rennie sit at a dark corner table of a plush restaurant. Menus and a quarter-full bottle of wine are in front of them, but no sign yet of food.

"So you're not completely opposed to faculty–student socializing, and *maybe* more?" Josie says, while under the table her un-shod foot seeks his.

"Not completely opposed, but wary," Rennie replies. "It cost me my first marriage."

He starts to reach for the bottle, stops himself, and pushes it further away

"Do you stay in touch?" asks Josie.

"With my ex-wife, yes; with the student, no."

"Do you see her often?"

"Oh, yes, we're good friends now. She works in the Registrar's Office."

Josie's eyes widen. "Millicent?"

"Yes, Millie."

"She seems sort of…" Josie stops abruptly. Then starts again, "I hope it's okay to say this."

Rennie reaches over and takes her hand. He smiles at her. "I can't imagine the Josie I know from the classroom hesitating to say *anything* to *anyone*."

Slowly she turns to look at him.

"I've only seen her a couple of times," she says, "but she seems kind of...haunted."

"We both are," he says.

"You two must have gone through a rough patch."

"It took a few years to work it through."

"Yes, it takes time," says Josie, a far-away look in her eyes. "I shouldn't say *this* either…"

He smiles again.

"But lots of relationships don't work out," says Josie. "Especially for my generation."

"I don't see you as from a different generation," says Rennie.

"From a different planet, maybe?" says Josie. "In the spirit of complete disclosure, I lived with a guy for three years and then one day he just walked out."

"Ouch," says Rennie.

Josie smiles and says, "I *can* imagine Rennie the professor using 'ouch' to indicate emotional pain."

"How did *you* feel?" asks Rennie.

"I felt like shit."

"That's the classroom Josie I remember."

"The day after he left, I went to the animal shelter and picked out a dog."

"The dirty-mouthed but practical Josie," says Rennie.

She slowly reaches over to move the now almost empty bottle even further from his grasp.

"Millie and I began seeing a couples counselor," says Rennie. "Professionally, that is. We weren't both having an *affair* with Sigmund."

Josie giggles.

"Millie thought we might try to live together for a while, and I didn't really want to, but then…" Rennie starts to sob.

Josie reaches for his hand, then pulls him to her and hugs him tightly.

Rennie starts to get control of himself. He is completely still for a moment.

He says softly, "Then our son Joe was killed in a drive-by shooting."

Josie gasps. *I didn't know they had them back then.* She says, "That must have been awful. I'm so sorry."

"Joe wasn't involved with gangs or drugs," says Rennie. "Just in the wrong place at the wrong time."

It fits together now, sort of, why he kept calling Dusty "Joe" and took such an interest in his family.

"We had a final session with Sigmund," says Rennie.

"Millie thought we should get back together, and so did Sigmund. I, instead, took a Josie-like approach to life."

Josie looks puzzled a moment, then asks, "What breed did you get?"

"Yorkshire Terrier," says Rennie.

"So you're starting to take my approach to life?"

"Well, in some ways, yes. Do you think there's a sexual relationship in the future for us?"

"You and the terrier?" She shrugs. "I won't vote anymore!"

"Fair enough," says Rennie, laughing. "I don't even know if creatures from your planet are allowed to vote on mine."

They both giggle.

The maitre d' passes by, escorting Bill and Emily to a table nearby.

"Now there's a couple everyone always *expected* to be together," says Josie. "Unlike us," she adds, perhaps a bit too loudly.

Bill, then Emily, Josie, and Rennie all blush. *In alphabetical order, as befits educators*, thinks Rennie.

When they are out of earshot, Bill says to Emily, "Rennie really seems to be attracted to Josie."

"And vice versa," says Emily. "It's often surprising the person we get attracted to."

He stares at her uncertainly, until she winks at him. "You think?" says Bill.

"Even more surprising is who we *stay* attracted to," says Emily, with another wink.

Reality Raises its Ugly Head

Bill's cell phone rings while he is driving home after a full day of teaching, topped off with three parent conferences. Emily is calling. He pulls off the road at the first safe opportunity and checks for a message.

Her usually relaxed voice sounds taut. "Bill, I must see you tonight about an urgent and important matter. Come over as soon as you can. I'll make dinner."

Bill immediately thinks, *But we've been so careful.* Outwardly calm, but inwardly shaken, he re-starts his car and rushes toward her apartment. He's glad he won't be eating alone.

He stops en route only to buy a paperback copy of *Expectant Fatherhood for Careless Dummies*.

He doesn't need to wait long to hear Emily's concern.

"They're trying to get me fired!" are Emily's opening words.

"Wow," he says. "Got some coffee brewed?"

"Over on the table there, next to my purse." She starts to detail the complaints now pouring in to her principal from both the American Legion and Gamblers Anonymous.

"You just need a good lawyer. Is anything else the matter?"

"No. But I will *not* let them fire me."

Bill senses he's said the wrong thing.

"In fact, I've decided to take a strong offensive action, and I want your support," says Emily.

Bill quickly glances over at Emily's purse looking for the outline of a handgun. W*hen she's this worked up,* w*ho knows what she's likely to do!*

"I'm going to run for Congress," she says.

"Gee, Em, that seems a little extreme. I want to help you, but let's start small. Can't your union help you out with this?"

"The union president is a golfing buddy of the principal, Bill."

"That could be a problem. But could we keep it local? If you have to run for something, why not start with the Board of Education?"

"Because they only have an election if there's a vacancy. Or somebody retires. Or dies."

Bill sneaks another glance at Emily's purse.

"Probably of boredom," she continues. "Then the mayor chooses a replacement. Look, I've thought this through. I'm going the Congress route."

"Hold on a minute, Em. Your principal gives you, a beginning teacher, some advice on how and how *not* to motivate your class. You disregard that advice.

"That could be a big problem for you, especially since you don't have tenure. But it's not a federal issue. Even if you ran and got elected, it's not something Congress is going to drop everything to help you out on."

"Bill, do you remember a recent president who used the slogan 'No Child Left Behind' to help him get elected and re-elected? What was *his* classroom experience? Reading stories to kindergarten kids on 9/11?

"I may be a beginning teacher, but I *am* a trained, certified teacher with a responsibility to do my best for my class.

"And at least half of Rennie's class really liked the idea of using lotteries instead of elections to choose members of Congress.

As a candidate, I'll have more opportunities to get out my message, *our* message. Just the novelty of raising this election vs. lottery issue in the primary will draw lots of free publicity."

"I'd like to help you, Em, but…"

"Good." She reaches into her purse. "I've got something for you." She pulls out a notebook and some papers.

"Your first assignment is to gather signatures. Lots of signatures."

"Well, uh, how many?"

"I've decided to run as a major-party candidate. In our last election, no Democratic or Republican candidate in any of our nine Congressional districts received *fewer* than 76,000 votes. But no third-party candidate got as *many* as 15,000."

"We have a third party here in Indiana?"

"Yes, Libertarians," Emily says. "If you're really interested in third parties, we should move to California. I've always wanted to. They've got…"

"No, no, that's okay. How many signatures do you want me to get?" He starts moving his lips and counting on his fingers as Emily shuffles through her notebook.

"We need only" She looks down at her notes, "500."

Two days later

Emily whispers to Bill, “How many?”

“Just seven,” he replies, in a somewhat louder whisper. “And you?”

“None. I’ve been working on fund-raising,” says Emily. She looks around. “This might not be the time or place to discuss it.”

Bill tries to keep what he’s feeling off his face and out of his voice. “Okay, 493 to go. That’s to reach the minimum and hope that none are declared invalid. I’ve about run out of friends and relatives. And even my friendly neighbors now don’t open their doors to me when I knock.”

From her rostrum at the front of the room, the Chair of the district-wide curriculum committee notices Bill and Emily’s intense conversation, and others intently clicking away on small electronic devices. “Let’s take a twenty-minute break,” she says.

Bill and Emily sit at a café and try to sort out their situation.

“After all we explored and learned in Rennie’s class, it’s ironic that we’re trying to use the old system of elections to get you into office,” says Bill.

“Ironic and difficult. And sad.” Emily sighs. “But what else is there right now?”

Bill is thoughtful. “California?”

Emily is surprised.

He says, “Let’s cut out to your place now and work on this in the morning.”

The next morning, after several cups of coffee.

"Get any sleep?" asks Bill.

"Not really. About two, I gave up and went on the internet.

"I couldn't get California out of my mind," says Emily. "Do you know that in their last election for President they had candidates on the ballot from the Democratic, Republican, Libertarian, Green, Peace and Freedom, and American Independent parties?"

Bill shakes his head.

"Who were the Peace and Freedom candidates?"

"Roseanne Barr for President and Cindy Sheehan for Vice-President.

"And seven other candidates not on the ballot also got write-in votes, with one of them getting over *twenty-one thousand!*"

"It's still the old system, but it looks like there's some good energy out there," says Bill.

The little engine that could

"Who do we allow to vote? Do we prevent many people who have a stake in the results from casting ballots? And who gets on the ballot?" asks Alice.

The class is startled by her unusually loud, clear voice. They are also surprised that Rennie does not introduce her and the topic of her term paper.

"We spend a lot of money to select the candidates, and millions more to elect them."

She is aware that her legs are shaking. She hopes the class doesn't notice.

"The process goes on for months."

Was it a mistake to do this without notes? No, it is an oral presentation and I can do it!

"The lives of *some* of us will be greatly affected. Others may not even notice the results. And if they do, they will soon forget."

She glances at Rennie, who smiles encouragingly.

"And before we know it, a new cycle will start."

She glances at Josie. She has not told her best friend in the class anything about her term paper or her oral presentation. Josie appears spellbound.

"How do the candidates feel at the moment the results are announced? The long hours put in, away from family and friends, the constant travel, the ever-present fear of misspeaking, of being caught by a photographer or TV cameraperson in an unflattering pose or unguarded moment? One careless slip in a long campaign could cost the election!

"And what about their associates, the behind-the-scenes people who worked on their campaigns? The pressures on them may be at least as great, the potential rewards much less, and even more uncertain.

"Wouldn't it really be better to have all the candidates' names on slips of paper and have the winner chosen by a lottery? It would be simpler, quicker, and cheaper.

"Who ultimately bears the cost of elections? Does the public ever know the cost? And why do we allow confusing ballots that include candidates for positions that we don't really care about?"

She takes a deep breath.

"I have been speaking today, of course, about the Academy Awards."

Most of the class looks very puzzled.

"Might anything I've said apply to a different situation?" says Alice, smiling.

Then Dusty stands up. "Brilliant!" he exclaims.

"You hit a walk-off home run!" shouts Benjamin.

"Go, girl, go!" shouts Josie, even louder.

They are all on their feet now, applauding wildly, even those who are still confused by Alice's last comment.

"Well done, Alice," says Rennie. "I knew you could pull it off."

"Thank you, everyone," says Alice. "Please sit down now. I've only just started.

"Now that I have your attention, let's discuss what the costs of electing our House of Representatives are, and who ultimately pays them.

"And by 'discuss,' I mean I want to hear *your* comments and questions, too."

What if it happened to *you*?

"What would you feel and do if *you* were chosen by lottery to be the next Representative in Congress from your district?" asks Jim at the start of his presentation.

"Three weeks ago, I stood by the door and handed out my questionnaire on my topic as you left this lecture room. It did not require your signature.

"Two weeks ago, I left a basket at the front of the classroom for you to return completed questionnaires.

"Today I'd like to share the results I got, offer some background information I think will be of interest, and offer *you* a chance to comment or ask questions.

"Fifty-four are registered in this class. I got 47 responses, which I understand is an excellent return rate in comparable contexts."

"I've never been in a class like this before," says Dusty. "So forget about 'comparable contexts' and just accept that we like you."

"This *is* a great class," "We learn together, and we support each other," says Alice.

"One week you blocked my leaving the classroom if I didn't take a blank survey," says Benjamin. "And the following week you barred me from coming in until I gave back a completed one."

Some teachers start to squirm and look around at others to see if they have had similar reactions.

Benjamin looks around too, smiles, and says, "I was just kidding."

Jim smiles too. *I never know if he's serious.*

"Eighty percent of the class said they would accept winning a seat as a Representative in Congress, 15% said they would decline, and 4% (one person) said, 'Wouldn't happen. I never win anything,'" says Jim.

"Why did you choose this topic?" asks Emily.

"Well, I'm probably the oldest person in the room," says Jim. "I was born in 1956."

Most look around the room, and their eyes rest on Rennie.

Rennie points to himself, "1960."

"Well," says Jim, "in 1975, at age 19, I was faced with a decision I think none of you have had to make.

"In that year, the U.S. Selective Service first used a lottery to determine the order in which men would be drafted into the Armed Forces, and probably sent to Vietnam. 'Lottery tickets' were based on the month and day of the year of their birth, as registered in the Selective Service records.

"That's when I 'won' the lottery. People born on my birth date, January 5th, were very high on the list to be drafted early. I didn't want to go to Vietnam to kill people I'd never even met. So I 'lost' when I 'won.'

"The question then for me was, should I *accept* the draft or *evade* it? I took immediate action to minimize my loss. I chose to evade it. I moved to Canada before I received my induction notice. I returned to the States in 1977, when President Jimmy Carter offered relatively lenient amnesties."

"Did many people avoid the draft? What happened to them?" asks Emily.

"Well, women avoided the draft by being women," says Jim. "The draft didn't apply to them. As for the men, you could look the topic up on *Wikipedia.com* to find out more.

"I've gotten some distance now from the events of the turbulent sixties. I can only say that I followed my conscience in moving to Canada, and I returned when I was ready.

"In writing this term paper, I thought that if *you* got a *seat in Congress* by winning the lottery, *you'd* have to make a major decision in *your* life. Should you accept it? What would you consider in deciding?

This assumes that we did switch from *election* to *lottery*, and you became a 'winner.' The first is what I hope for, and the second is highly unlikely for any one of us. But as a teaching tool, it's useful to speculate about.

"And we are all teachers."

Rennie smiles. *And you, Jim, are a particularly good one*.

Jim thinks *I got a little long-winded there*. He says,

"My questionnaire asked what positive and negative factors you'd take into account in making that decision. This slide shows some of the interesting answers I got.

"In some cases, I've simplified the syntax and corrected the spelling. Couldn't help myself. Just part of the double major in History and English I got as an undergraduate."

Jim reads aloud what's on the slide.

What factors might you consider when you decide?

Positive
High salary
Prestige
High pension after only a one-year stint
Excellent health plan benefits
It might be an interesting job in itself!
An opportunity for advancement (The Presidency!)
Make contacts to get good position in private sector
Foreign travel at government expense
Summers off, just like in teaching!
We could keep our summer cottage.

Negative
Hot and humid in Washington DC
High crime rate
Difficult adjustment for my family

Might be Positive or Negative
Whether my husband could also get a job in DC

Would you move to a new state just *because* it had switched from an election to lottery system?

Depends on which state
Would my family and I be happy in Washington?
Well, it would give me a chance every two years to win the lottery without ever buying a ticket
I wouldn't want to

If you moved to a state that switched to a lottery system and still kept the same major parties, which party would you join?

Whichever was the majority party

I've been in a minority group all my life. I'm left-handed, something that's hard to change. It's an advantage in some sports. Don't know about politics. Might be tempted to see what life in a majority group is like.

I'd like to stay clear of both

They might have a third party that attracted me. If not, I might start one

"That's been very thought provoking, Jim," says Rennie. "And I'm sure many here would like to add their comments. But we only have so much time. Can someone here set up a blog site, or whatever you call those internet things, for our class to make its comments available? If so, see me afterwards.

"For now, Jim, please move *briefly* into the second part of your presentation."

"Sure," says Jim. "This draws upon the other half of my double major. I call it, "The Role of the Lottery in History, Governmental Actions, Higher Education, Literature and Film.

"My next slide shows some situations in which lotteries have been used to select people:

The Lottery in History

In Athens in the Fourth Century BC, lawmakers and jurors were frequently chosen by lot. There were limits on how long they could serve.

The U.S. Government

The Census bureau decides by lot which citizens to give the long or short census form to fill out.

The government uses a lottery to choose among applicants for some temporary residence visas.

Governments of Other Countries

Some pilgrims get visas to travel to Saudi Arabia for the Hajj pilgrimage when chosen by lottery.

Local Government Use

Many states use a random drawing based upon car or voter registrations to select jurors.

Higher Education Selection of Students

Some colleges and universities base admissions of new students in part upon random drawing.

Literature

In the story *The Lottery*, by Shirley Jackson, the villagers use a lottery to choose who will be stoned to death each year for ceremonial purposes.

Cinema

In *The Hunger Games*, two teenagers from each district of a fictitious country are chosen at random to compete in a televised fight to the death.

"In summary, to echo Emily and Bill's class talk, why not choose our representatives Congress by lottery?

"Any questions, comments?" asks Jim.

Almost every hand is raised.

"I don't know who to call on first," says Jim. "Good time for a lottery."

Rennie steps forward quickly.

"Thank you, Jim. A very interesting presentation. Again, if anyone knows how to set up a blog-thingy for us so we can all share comments and Jim can answer your questions, please let me know.

"But right now I need to bring up a different topic."

Worried looks appear on some faces in the class.

"We've got a time problem. Some of you have not yet arranged with me the topic of your term project, or have started working on the project but may not be on track to finish by the end of the semester."

A number of students start to squirm in their seats, and look around for others in the same situation.

"If this applies to you, please see me about how we can make sure you satisfy the course requirements.

"I've told you that you will determine your letter grade in this course and I stand by that. But I hope you will avoid the 'incomplete' option.

"I hastily threw together this course upon the death of Professor Leonard, and I see now how negligent I was in planning it.

"From grade school through graduate school, I was asked to do many 'projects.' But I can't remember any instructor telling me the *purpose* of those projects.

"I realize *I* never discussed with you the purpose of the term project and class presentation for this course. Let me briefly do that now.

"As schoolteachers, you are trained how to impart knowledge and skills to students. But your job also entails working with your colleagues on committees to exchange information, make decisions, and solve problems together.

"And if you leave teaching for another line of work, or if you have already worked in other settings before teaching, you will soon learn, or know already, that communicating with colleagues is an important but seldom taught skill.

"Alice and Jim's presentations have shown how flexible I can be in approving your choices of topics and of presentation format.

"Please take advantage of my flexibility to meet your course responsibilities and to better prepare yourself for your current and future jobs."

"May I say something here, Rennie?" says Arthur.

Did Rennie mislead the class?

"You've misled us, Rennie," says Arthur.

The class becomes completely silent. No more constant undercurrent of whispered conversation. No restless body movements, just eyes shifting focus back and forth between Arthur standing in front, and Rennie, seated a few feet away from him at his right.

The class suppresses its gasps of surprise as long as possible. Then slightly muffled coughs are heard.

Rennie watches Arthur intently, but shows no emotion.

"This isn't a summary of my term paper I handed in on the topic we agreed upon," continues Arthur. "This is the result of too many sleepless nights I spent, watching TV news programs and listening to talking heads on panels tell me what's going on in this world."

He turns to Rennie. "May I continue?"

"Please do," says Rennie.

"You call this course *Starting a Country from Scratch: Re-Forming the United States of America*.

"Catchy title. But there is no *scratch* here. There's a *country* here that's been in existence for hundreds of years, and that has a constitution, a legislative body, and a judiciary.

"And it's made up of smaller units called 'states.' It has traditions, bureaucrats, civil service employees, organized pressure groups, highly paid lobbyists, long established political parties, and organized crime.

"You've encouraged some members of the class to propose we use a lottery to replace elections as a way to select our House of Representatives.

"They made persuasive arguments for doing so. And I agree with them. But that's not the question we should pursue now.

"The real question now is, if we want to switch from an *election* to a *lottery* system, *how* can we peacefully make this transition?

"After my sleepless week of watching TV and reading about events in Egypt, Afghanistan, Syria, Turkey, Lebanon, Pakistan and Iraq, I haven't seen anything about any third-world countries clamoring for our help in redesigning their governments. And you told us at the beginning of the course that they would ask for our help and that we should be prepared to give it.

"I started by saying you misled us, and I was wrong. Please accept my apology.

"I know that as a businessman you try to predict future trends, but sometimes you're wrong, things happen you can't predict or control, and you adjust your plan.

"You didn't mislead us, you just made a wrong prediction.

"I know that you didn't plan to teach this course or any course, but an unexpected death led to your being offered the opportunity, and you accepted.

"And I'll say this too. This has been the most stimulating course I've ever taken. Anywhere.

"I can't believe it's offered in a School of Education."

Some laughter, boos, and applause.

Rennie gets up to reply.

"Thanks, Arthur, for those appropriate, from-the-heart remarks. You had the insight to identify a key problem in what we've been doing, and the courage to bring it up publicly.

"You started by saying I've misled you. It was true. And by saying that, you created an alert audience for your message that followed.

"Go home now and get some sleep. When you're rested, start remembering the applause and laughter, and think about the grade for yourself that you'll be handing me in a sealed envelope at the end of the course."

Arthur and Rennie rush toward each other and hug.

"You're an oddball, Rennie," calls out Josie. "But a loveable oddball."

A party that's needed

"*I'm* first?" says Dusty. "Why do I go first?"

"Because as MC, I'm making up the rules," says Alice, who gulped down a drink right after the last class of the semester ended half an hour ago as the party began. "And because you were so supportive of me when I panicked just before I gave my oral report about my term paper, and I've sort of fallen in love with you."

Hoots, laughs, and applause. Alice is a bit flustered.

Her friend Emily intercedes. "Alice, before Dusty exercises his well-earned right to go first, could Bill and I make a brief announcement?"

That quiets the crowd. "Of course," says Alice, both relieved and intensely curious. "Please do. And it doesn't have to be brief." She looks around. "I don't see anyone around here young enough to be under a curfew."

"Thanks, Alice." Emily takes Bill's hand, and the two of them move to where everyone can see them.

"We're leaving for California tomorrow," she says.

A very brief moment of stunned silence. Then questions come pouring out from all sides.

"A vacation trip?"

"No," says Emily. "We intend to live there."

"What will you both do there?"

"In California, they have political parties like Libertarian, Green, Peace and Freedom, and American Independent.

"We plan to attend their events, get opportunities to talk to the members, suggest to them that a lottery may be a better way of choosing representatives than elections, and learn what they can teach us from their experiences being in minor parties. Maybe we can all work together toward a 'lottery revolution.'"

"Why are you leaving so soon?"

"Once we decided on what we wanted to do, we got itchy to get going," chimes in Bill.

"Are you driving out there?"

"Yes," say Emily and Bill together. "Anyone want to share the driving, the expenses, and the fun?" adds Emily.

"If tomorrow is too sudden for you, we could maybe wait a day or two while you wind up your affairs," says Bill. "Right, Em?"

"Well, no more than two days," she replies.

Emily and Bill smile at Alice.They stroll away, as Bill sings, "Get your kicks, on Route 66."

Alice smiles, then looks over to Dusty. "Okay, you can be first now. Tell us what *your* plans are."

"Okay, I'm first." He looks over at Alice, winks at her, and shrugs in mock resignation to his unfortunate situation.

"Anyway, the question was what I am going to do next. I've applied to law school. Actually to five law schools. I may not get into any of them.

"It's a long process, and I only recently decided on it. I need to complete the applications, get transcripts sent out, take admission tests, and make sure my letters of recommendation go out on time."

He looks over at Rennie. "In the meantime, I'll take Rennie's next course this coming semester, *Field Work in Alternative Political Organizing.*"

Rennie thinks, *I really did do a good job with the boy!*

"Actually," says Rennie, "I probably won't be teaching that new course this coming year."

"Why not?" shout out several party-goers at the same time.

"What will you be doing?" asks Josie, trying to hide the sudden panic she feels.

Rennie looks quickly around the room for anyone recording video on their cell phone. He asks, "Is anybody recording this?"

"No, we're all with you," says Arthur.

"I'll ditto that," says Jim.

"Well," says Rennie, "I told you about my meeting with the Dean, and his suggestion that I broker a deal between Emily, her principal, and the complaining parents. And that, in return, he'd go out of his way to help me advance in my professional career."

"No! You didn't sell her out!" says Alice.

"No, of course not.

"I proposed a deal that he accepted, but it's certainly nothing like the one he wanted.

"I reminded him that *he* was the one who organized the Super Bowl Lottery and strongly coerced faculty participation, saying 'A certain percentage of all funds collected will go to a deserving senior who otherwise would be unable to attend our graduate school.'

"He never told us that 'certain percentage' was two percent.

"I told him the University's Board of Trustees, if they knew of this, might be worried about bad publicity, law suits, Congressional investigations, and so forth.

"I can imagine, I told him, that a good chunk of the money taken in went into the Registrar's discretionary funds for trips to Europe to recruit students, usually accompanied by his private secretary, just in case letters needed to be typed."

"How did you know all this?" asks Alice.

"Well," says Rennie, "when he suddenly 'relieved me of all teaching responsibilities' for allowing students to grade themselves, he forgot to relieve me of my committee assignments. And sometimes members of the Financial Oversight Committee remembered to invite me to its meetings.

"Especially when the Dean was 'out of town on business.'

"I told him that Millicent in the Registrar's Office has considerable responsibility for a wide range of matters, which she carries out quite competently, and that she hasn't had a pay raise in three years, while a certain secretary in *his* office, with no known *official* responsibilities and a large unaccounted-for travel budget, now earns almost twice what Millicent earns.

"He became livid. But he didn't deny anything.

"To his credit, he seems to learn from experience. He was just silent for an uncomfortable few moments.

"Uncomfortable for him.

"I told him I consulted a lawyer friend of mine last night, who told me that what Emily teaches or doesn't teach is no business of this university, and that an anonymous letter has no legal status. He also said if the parent really existed, came forward, *and* was willing to attest to the facts, this would result in a barrage of lawsuits, subpoenas and other legal investigations.

"I told him the lawyer said that the University would immediately 'retire' any employee *such as you, Gerald,* who dragged it into unfavorable publicity that might result in a decline in alumni contributions. And that, ultimately, the press would label the employee an 'un-American trouble-maker.'"

"Is that truly what would happen?" asks Dusty.

"I have no idea," says Rennie.

"But neither did the Dean. And he didn't want to find out.

"I told him, that was the deal, take it or leave it."

"But that's what the lawyer told you?" asks Dusty.

"Actually, there is no lawyer yet, but he's applied to five law schools and I'm confident..."

Rennie is interrupted by howls and applause.

Dusty looks up and smiles at Rennie, and joins in the applause.

"You out-bluffed him, Rennie!" says Josie.

"I'd hate to play poker with you, man!" says Benjamin.

When the noise dies down, Arthur asks, "So what do *you* get in the deal?"

"I'll explain the deal in a few moments," says Rennie.

"First, let me suggest what some of you might do if the course I've made preliminary plans for, *Field Work in Alternative Political Organizing*, appeals to you.

"You might get together in the next two weeks to sketch out more details of the objectives and methods of the course, and a plan to recruit students to take it. Then rush to the Dean for his advice on modifying the plan and request funding from him to implement it.

"Right now is the best time to contact him. He's highly motivated to please my former students and me. The sooner you meet with him, the better. Before he makes a misstep and gets fired."

"Could you share some details of your preliminary plans with us tonight?" asks Dusty. "Then we could get started right away. Or rather, as soon as we sober up."

He sneaks a look at Alice.

Rennie laughs. "By 'preliminary plans' I meant I came up with the title."

Antoine laughs. "Well, it is a bit vague. Sort of like your sign when we saw it written the first day of class."

STARTING A COUNTRY FROM SCRATCH: Re-Forming the United States of America

Rennie smiles. He recalls the first day vividly. His mind flashes over many scenes from the past semester.

How Emily and Bill taught him the meaning of 'dry erase board'...

He blinks, and forces himself to return to the present and to consider the future.

"Well," he says, "in the two days after Professor Leonard's tragic death, about all I could manage was to come up with a course title. Here's your chance to get in right at the beginning under more pleasant circumstances.

"You've been a wonderful group to work with. I'm sorry that, due to various interruptions, we haven't had the time for everyone to give their oral report to the class.

"If you can arrange it, I'd suggest an informal brainstorming session on the challenging topic that Arthur so recently presented us with, 'How can we peacefully make the transition from an *election* to a *lottery* system?'

"That could be a good starting point to plan the new course.

"Now, the details of the deal.

"First of all, Millicent will get a large salary increase, retroactive for two years, to be taken from the other 98% of the lottery ticket sales. She got her first back-payment on Friday.

"And the Dean had promised to use his foundation contacts to get me back into academia. Remember, I was just on a temporary emergency contract. So I told him to get me a two-year fellowship studying governmental reform in Canada."

"*Canada*?" exclaims Jim.

"I know you lived there during the Vietnam War and for a while afterward. And you, Antoine, grew up there."

"And I was in Niagara Falls on my honeymoon," adds Gregory.

"Well," says Rennie, "I've been trying to follow the political situation there. When we started our course, I thought we'd look at basic needed changes in the U.S. government structure, then apply what we'd learned to help Middle Eastern countries.

"But it doesn't look now that they want our help, and it might not be safe for the class members to go there even if they were invited in."

"But *Canada*?" asks Josie.

"Some Canadians want to get rid of the Senate, the upper house of their Parliament.

"And well, there's a lot of opposition to that, especially among the Senators themselves, who are not elected(!), but *appointed* by the Prime Minister, who *is* elected. In a complicated way, that is at least as screwy as how *we* elect our President!

"I reminded the Dean to compensate me for my arranging the settlement, as he had promised to assist me in my next career decision. I told him to arrange with his good friends at rich foundations to get me the two-year fellowship in Canada."

"Where in Canada would you want to live?" asks Josie.

"Well, I think my years among the American cornfields have been enough for me. I'm ready for some big city life.

"And he's come through with a rent-free three bedroom house in Montreal, and a reasonable stipend to live on."

"Is *that* where you want to live in Canada?" asks Josie.

"I spent a week there a long time ago. It's rather nice. French culture. Delicious food. European atmosphere."

"Delicious French cooking?" asks Josie.

"Oh, yes! And other good European and Asian cuisines too. But as I remember it, you should stay away from the poutine."

"You *can* develop a taste for it. I did," says Antoine.

"*Three* bedrooms?" says Josie.

"Yes, I thought one for me, one to serve as an office, and one if a visitor came.

"Would you like to visit me there, Josie?"

The end.
And maybe a new beginning.

CPSIA information can be obtained at www.ICGtesting.com
Printed in the USA
LVOW11s0600121114

413165LV00001B/1/P

9 781632 631442